China's Urban Transition

China's Urban Transition

John Friedmann

UNIVERSITY OF MINNESOTA PRESS

MINNEAPOLIS • LONDON

All photographs in the book were taken by Daniel Abrahamson.

Maps were designed by Eric Leinberger.

Published by the University of Minnesota Press
111 Third Avenue South, Suite 290
Minneapolis, MN 55401-2520
http://www.upress.umn.edu

Library of Congress Cataloging-in-Publication Data

Friedmann, John.
    China's urban transition / John Friedmann.
        p. cm.
    Includes bibliographical references and index.
    ISBN 0-8166-4614-7 (hc : alk. paper) — ISBN 0-8166-4615-5 (pb : alk. paper)
1. Urbanization—China. 2. Local government—China. 3. Civil society—China.
4. China—Economic conditions—2000- I. Title.

    HT384.C6F75 2005
    307.76'0951—dc22

                                            2004022458

Printed in the United States of America on acid-free paper

The University of Minnesota is an equal-opportunity educator and employer.

12 11 10 09 08 07 06   10 9 8 7 6 5 4 3 2

For Martin
globetrotter and maestro extraordinaire

Contents

Preface

The current "transition" to urbanism in China is taking place within an ancient tradition. Although most people who have not visited the country may still think of China as an essentially rural society, the documented history of its cities goes back to China's imperial beginnings and includes not just a handful but hundreds of cities. This history is very different from the European experience. In Europe, which has an urban tradition of similar antiquity centered on the Mediterranean, cities were often city-states; China's cities, well marked in the landscape by imposing walls, never developed institutions of self-governance. For the most part, Chinese cities were seats of imperial power rather than powers in their own right.

Still, the tradition of urbanism in China offers no precedent for the scale of the current transition. Already today, more than one-third (36 percent) of the population of China lives in cities, and the proportion continues to increase year by year: within another thirty years, nearly two-thirds (60 percent or more) of China's citizens will live in cities, a rise from approximately 460 million to 900 million. This is a story of both transition and profound transformation, a story that by dint of its sheer dimensions cannot be ignored.

But there is another compelling reason for studying China's urban transformation. Many foreign observers are captivated by glossy pictures of Shanghai's gleaming office towers and luxury hotels, images that suggest yet another global metropolis in the making (not only in Shanghai but in other Chinese megacities as well). Such images contribute to the widely held belief that the country is racing to be globalized, to "catch up" with the West. This belief is often reinforced by the Chinese themselves, who are proud to point to these symbols of their country's modernization. But this picture obscures the sociocultural processes actually at work in China and deeply embedded in its history. China, it is useful to recall, is more than a nation-state; it is also one of the world's great civilizations. In this respect, it is the equivalent of western Europe or India and can be expected to develop in ways and directions that are not part of the Western repertoire of experience. This makes the "reading" of China a fascinating exploration. For this reason, throughout this volume, I will comment on China's unique approach while examing such topics as the question of urban governance, the role of "civil society," or the extent to which the achievements of the reform era are a result of developments from within rather than an offshoot of globalization.

This volume is an introduction to China's multiple urbanization processes during the reform era. It is intended for students, scholars, and others who are not China specialists but have an interest in understanding the recent past and who may seek a guide to the current literature. My background is in urban and regional planning, and I have had a lifelong interest in cities and their genesis, growth, and regional impacts. This book attempts to synthesize and interpret the pertinent English-language literature. Although there are a number of magisterial books on Chinese cities by single authors, recent writings on urbanization are found scattered in specialized journal articles and in the chapters of multiauthor volumes that are often reworked conference proceedings. Some of these writings have an almost journalistic flavor, and many lack historical perspective. Given the widespread fascination with the rapid pace of the urban transition, this is perhaps inevitable. At the same time, many of these accounts are little more than vignettes that will acquire a historical patina before long. Often they are essentially snapshots taken at a single point in time that will soon acquire the feel of a distant, bygone era. This, for instance, is the impression one gets from reading Ross Terrill's "portraits" of cities in his book *Flowers on an Iron Tree* (1975). Terrill is a perceptive traveler, but the images he paints of Shanghai, Dalian, Hangzhou, Wuhan, and Beijing toward the end of the Maoist era strike a more contemporary traveler as coming from another century. And yet, the time that has elapsed is less than thirty years!

Friends have asked me why I have chosen to devote years of my official retirement from the University of California at Los Angeles to a study of China's urbanization. Besides a lifelong personal interest in Chinese philosophy and poetry, there are other reasons that, I hope, will stir the interest of readers as much as they have motivated my own investment of time. What is happening in China today is, I would argue, of world-historical importance. Over the past century, China has emerged as a major economic power in

Asia. It is now a relatively stable polity undergoing rapid and sustained economic growth, one of the world's largest industrial producers. Within a decade or two, it will also have scientific and technical abilities to rival those of the most advanced nations. Geographically, it shares borders with India, Nepal, Bhutan, Pakistan, Tajikistan, Kyrgyzstan, Kazakhstan, the Russian Federation, Mongolia, North Korea, Vietnam, Laos, and Myanmar. It is a near neighbor to the Republic of Korea and to Japan. Unquestionably, China is already the most powerful and dynamic country in this region.

I am deeply indebted to my good friends and colleagues—Timothy Cheek, Michael Leaf, Timothy Brook, Daniel Abramson, and Heng Chye Kiang— who took the time and trouble to read a draft of this text in its entirety and offered trenchant comments and suggestions that greatly helped me improve the present version. In addition, Mee Kam Ng commented perceptively on chapter 6. I am particularly grateful to Daniel Abramson for allowing me to use his splendid images of the urban transition in China and to Eric Leinberger for his beautiful cartography. Last but not least, I wish to acknowledge the careful editing of Lys Ann Shore, whose sensitive feel for language greatly improved the readability of my text.

The love of my life, Leonie Sandercock, not only read every line of this book in the making, but kept up my spirits throughout this long adventure in more ways than she will ever know.

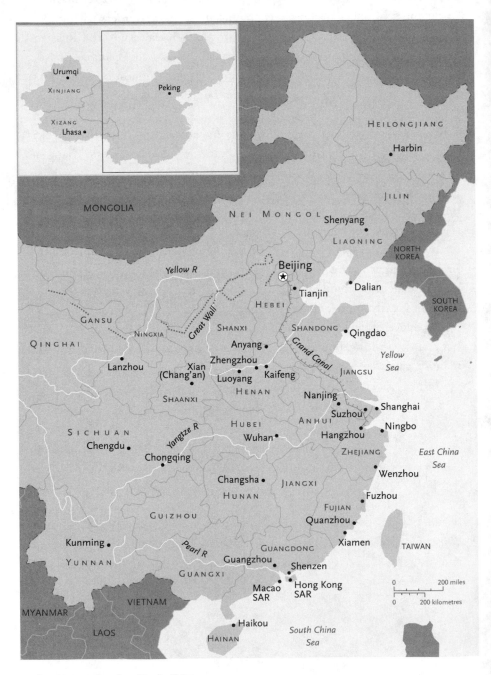

Provinces and major cities in China

Introduction: Becoming Urban in China

At the start of the twentieth century, China launched upon an epic journey, whose trajectory remains incomplete, and whose ultimate outcome is imponderable. After a reign of 255 years, the foreign Manchu dynasty finally collapsed in 1911. The Manchu rulers had proven unable to deal successfully with the new political forces in the world, forces from which China was no longer exempt. The following year in Nanjing, Sun Yat-sen inaugurated the Republic.

The next three decades are years of unimaginable turmoil as warlords struggle for regional dominance. Japanese armies invade China, set up a puppet state in Manchuria, and then, turning south, conquer Shanghai and Nanjing. Meanwhile, the Guomindang (nationalist) government under Chiang Kai-shek, with only a tenuous hold on the country, is locked in a bitter civil war with communist irredentists led by Mao Zedong. In the end, the Japanese are defeated, the nationalist government retreats to its last bastion in Taiwan, and standing on Tiananmen Square on October 1, 1949, Mao Zedong proclaims the People's Republic of China, ushering in three decades of revolutionary communism. A system of central planning, Soviet-style, replaces the market economy, while a process of forced-march industrialization is begun, favoring heavy industry. Less than ten years later, in 1958, agricultural household production is collectivized under the system of people's communes, and 500 million peasants are mobilized to produce the surpluses needed for investment in the new state-owned industries. Mass mobilizations for utopian projects during the Great Leap Forward and the Cultural Revolution turn into calamities, but Mao himself holds on to power until his death in 1976. After a brief struggle against those who had inherited his mantle—the notorious Gang of Four—Deng Xiaoping rises to supreme power in 1978. He initiates a series of far-reaching reforms, beginning with the de-collectivization of agriculture, the first steps toward a socialist market economy, and China's opening to the world.[1]

The events just cited would surely form a grand narrative suggesting progressive, linear movement: from disunity to unity; from colonial subordination to autochthonous national development; from submissive weakness to assertive strength; from relative closure to the world to becoming part of the global "space of flows." Or movement from the stagnation, underdevelopment, and poverty of an agrarian society to the dynamic development of a diversified urban-industrial economy; from an archipelago of regions to an increasingly integrated national space economy; and from a predominantly village-based society to one that is increasingly urban. The main problem with composing a grand narrative from such differently slanted accounts of more or less the same sequence of events is that the story is still unfinished. We don't know its outcome or its larger significance in the context of China's millennial history, and the lack of distancing from events that crowd the pages of the daily press results in an absence of perspective that makes it difficult to say more than "this happened and then that." Will the story hold? Will it reverse itself? Will China triumph as a liberal democracy, or will its current rise to world power trigger yet another world conflagration? These and similar questions set limits to what we can say about China's recent past. Thus, our narrative remains truncated and will no doubt be subject to major rectification in the years to come.

My intention in this book is to write the story of China's accelerated urbanization, focusing on the last twenty-five years of post-Mao market reform. It is a multi-layered story. In its simplest, most familiar form, it refers to a shift in the proportion of total population that demographers have classified as rural as opposed to urban. In China, this has meant an increase in urban population from roughly 10 percent in 1949 to 36 percent fifty years later. Out of a current population of 1.3 billion, this yields a present-day total of about 470 million urban dwellers (Chan and Hu 2003). Demographic projections suggest that this upward trend is likely to continue for the next twenty-five years and beyond, by which time more than 50 percent of an even larger total population will be classified as urban—that is, as officially residing in cities as defined by the census. But in addition to this statistical definition, there are at least five other dimensions of "becoming urban" that embrace administrative, economic, physical, sociocultural, and political aspects.[2] When taken together, these constitute a dynamic matrix of forces that, alas, are not always fully synchronized. Urbanization is an uneven spatial process of leads and lags that inevitably produces social tensions, conflicts, and outbursts of popular protest.

Through the influence of the media, sociocultural urbanization spreads more rapidly these days than any of the other forms, stimulating desires that are difficult to restrain. Peasants launch themselves as instant entrepreneurs to start up new rural industries. Economic urbanization outruns the ability of local governments to provide for the necessary social infrastructure. Some regions urbanize early and, building on their success, leave less dynamic regions far behind. Migration brings peasants into cities, but when they return home, as many do, they carry with them a bit of the city into the countryside. Old concepts of community and solidarity are stretched to the limit as people strive to get ahead without bothering much over how others may be affected. And an accelerated process of economic and cultural change leads to a foreshortened view of life, where instant benefits are expected whatever their effects on the longer-term future. Important though it may be, the idea that urban development should be sustainable is of relatively little concern to those who want to get a foothold on the upward-bound escalator to the good life.

All these different dimensions must be read and understood in spatial terms. Relevant concepts, such as region, peri-urban areas, migration, boundaries, overspill, scale, space economy, human settlements, locality, and so forth, abound in the literature no less than in this book. And yet, most of the boundaries implied in so many spatial metaphors are porous, leading to different and often unexpected spatial configurations of the urban. Clearly, social and economic relations are no longer bounded. While this creates ambiguities, uncertainties, and confusion aplenty, it may also lead to the discovery of new opportunities for those who are willing to work within the shadow-land of unbounded practices that are largely devoid of state-made rules. The central state is naturally nervous about the proliferation of these spaces, of practices it can no longer control. But in the contemporary world, boundlessness is a fundamental condition of the multiplex phenomenon of urbanization, the genie that no state knows how to push back into the bottle.

Except during the first decade of revolutionary communism, when the country received a good deal of aid from the Soviet Union, Mao's China was a self-reliant, closed economy. Until the onset of the reforms in the late 1970s, both national and internal boundaries mattered a great deal. The city unbound is a phenomenon of the recent period when China became increasingly part of the "global space of flows" (Castells 1996). Since then, it has been customary to speak of urbanization as being strongly influenced by global capital, and even to speak of "global cities" and other such hierarchies (Sassen 1991; Friedmann 1986, 1998b). Some authors, such as John Logan, have even used globalization as a preferred perspective on Chinese urbanization (Logan 2002). And indeed some Chinese cities, such as Shanghai, Hong Kong, and Beijing, have announced plans to become "international" cities, which is the Chinese term for "world city." But I have decided to avoid this language, for several reasons. First, adopting globalization as the analytical framework for the study of cities tends to privilege outside forces to the neglect of internal visions, historical trajectories, and endogenous capabilities. It also places emphasis on economics to the exclusion of sociocultural and political variables. Finally, in China's case, it is not always easy to tell what is "inside" and what is "outside." So-called foreign investments, it turns out, come more often than not from Hong Kong and Taiwan, places whose actual status as "foreign" territories is moot. (The People's Republic of China insists on calling Taiwan a Chinese province, and Hong Kong was incorporated into China as a special administrative region in 1997.) Additional large amounts of "foreign" capital have come from the Chinese diaspora in Southeast Asia, Australia, California, and elsewhere, families that in many cases are only one or two generations removed from their ancestral villages. But if we look at the Chinese diaspora as an integral part of a "Greater China," what would otherwise be called a process of globalization suddenly turns into an endogenous process of a transnational China, a sort of "China unbound."[3] The great historian John King Fairbank comes to a similar conclusion: "As we have always suspected, China's center of gravity lay within, among the Chinese people, and that is where the ingredients of revolution accumulated" (Fairbank 1986, 62).

Instead of globalization, then, my perspective stresses urbanization as an evolutionary process that is driven from within, as a form of endogenous development. This has led me to take my starting points in China's history, which is not simply the history of a nation-state but the story of a civilization whose roots, as far as cities are concerned, reach back more than thirty-five hundred years. It is a civilization unified by a literary culture and by philosophical and religious traditions whose origins lie deep in antiquity. The cosmological philosophy of yin and yang—which is the unity of opposites—as developed in the text and commentaries of the *I Ching* or the *Book of Changes*, Confucian moral teachings, Daoist quietism, and the political realism of the Legalist tradition are the common heritage of all Chinese.[4] Over the course of history, China has been divided and unified, ruled by foreigners and self-governing. For centuries, it was a great sea-going trading power in the Pacific while maintaining an active commerce with Europe and Asia over inland routes. By the mid-fifteenth century, it returned to being a continental empire, more concerned with its relations to Central Asian polities than with overseas adventures.[5] A country on this scale, with an unbroken history of four millennia, and which today accounts for more than one out of every five human beings on Earth, perforce develops out of its own resources, traditions, and civilizational genius.

In chapter 1, therefore, I take a quick backward glance at the emergence of cities on the North China Plain thirty-five hundred years ago, following up with a sketch of Chang'an (present-day Xi'an), the imperial capital of the Sui and Tang dynasties between the sixth and tenth centuries of the present era. Chang'an was a splendid city, renowned the world over. It was also a tightly regulated city, whose population of perhaps a million people lived within the walled compounds inside the imposing city walls made of rammed earth that stretched for 37 km around the city. The compounds were regularly closed at nightfall, to be reopened only at dawn. High walls similarly enclosed the city's two markets, which drew merchants from all over China and beyond. Despite its magnificence, Chang'an looked in many ways like a military encampment. The urban historian Heng Chye Kiang contrasts the regimented life of this "city of aristocrats" with the more open, demotic city of Kaifeng, the imperial capital of the Northern Song, which flourished three centuries later, and whose busy life spilled out into its streets.

Leaping ahead, the same chapter pauses to explore nineteenth-century Hankou on the Yangzi River, which today has become integrated with the inland city of Wuhan that some would call China's Chicago. During the late Qing dynasty, Hankou was a major trading emporium. Originally without walls and therefore not an imperial city, it is of particular interest in the present context for the way its associational life maintained order in the city at large. Unlike the cities of Western Europe, Chinese cities generally, and Hankou in particular, were not corporate entities, and the idea of municipal self-government had not yet been invented in China. Order and essential services, such as fire brigades and a variety of welfare institutions, were maintained by merchant and gentry elites, sometimes in negotiations with the imperial government's representative in the nearest capital city.

The chapter concludes with a look at the city under Mao's regime of revolutionary communism. The tradition of the "open city," as represented by the examples of Kaifeng and Hankou, was abruptly cut short by a system of household registration that, in effect, tied every individual in China to his or her place of official residence, thus restraining migration, particularly to large cities. This so-called *hukou* system, albeit in modified form, persists to this day. As for the city proper, its basic building block became the *danwei* or work unit, which turned away from the street as a public space. With its walled compounds that brought together workers' residences with their places of work, the *danwei* recalled the regimented order of ancient Chang'an.

Chapter 2 provides some background to regional policies since 1949. Communist China, coming to power in the nuclear age, and having fought against the United States during the Korean War, felt beleaguered. Mao and his close associates who had fought alongside him during the years of revolutionary struggle and the war against Japan thought in military more than economic terms. The break with the Soviet Union in 1960 brought with it an additional potential threat on China's northern borders. In any event, the government adopted a regional policy called the Third Front strategy. Its aim was to render China's fledgling industries immune from attack by hiding them "in the mountains, in dispersion, and in caves" of the western regions, such as Sichuan Province. At the same time, each province was exhorted to become economically self-sufficient. Although industrial relocation was often highly inefficient, and the notion of regional self-sufficiency merely reinforced the preexisting character of China's landscape as an "archipelago" of regions, the strategy was justified on military grounds.

After coming to power in 1978, Deng Xiaoping reversed this strategy, replacing it with what was dubbed the "Ladder-Step Doctrine." Accordingly, the country was divided into three mega-regions: coastal, central, and western. Each mega-region was assigned specific tasks in the overall development of the country. Priority was given to the coastal provinces, which had the necessary infrastructure and human resources for a period of accelerated industrial expansion. In due course, a regional balance would be achieved, as economic growth moved, step by step, from coastal cities to the central and western regions. This policy of letting some regions get rich first would be undergirded by efforts to promote regional interdependencies. Breaking with the Maoist past, this approach would in the longer term achieve an integrated national space economy. As for cities, they would be "opened up" and become more like Kaifeng and Hankou, leaving the walls of the *danwei* to crumble from benign neglect. The prominence of the street would be reclaimed.

These policies highlighted ongoing developments in the two major delta regions of China, the Pearl and Yangzi Rivers. Chapter 2 concludes with a closer examination of one of these "restless landscapes" in China's current phase of development, raising a major question regarding the growing inequalities between rural and urban China and among its many diverse regions.

Chapter 3 focuses on the amazing upsurge of rural industries in the first two decades of the reform period, particularly in coastal provinces. In the late 1990s their output amounted to perhaps a third of China's industrial output overall. This has transformed villages and townships into what in sociocultural and physical terms are urban areas. Indeed, many counties that urbanized spontaneously were subsequently raised to city status. The emphasis in this chapter is on their endogenous development. Here, too, historical factors were decisive, such as century-old craft traditions like ceramics or silk. Rural industrialization in the contemporary sense had its beginning during the revolutionary period, when it formed an important source of side income for communes that were otherwise centered on the production of grain and small livestock. The dissolution of the communes and the return to the household system of production led to an unprecedented and, indeed, unexpected outburst of local entrepreneurship. A series of miniature case studies helps to bring to life this transformation of rural areas, a transformation that seems to have happened helter-skelter in an incredibly short period of time. Some of the new enterprises were privately owned, some were organized as share-holding companies, but the majority were managed collectively—that is, they were held by the village or township in common.

Much of chapter 3 details six conditions that favored this unique process of urbanizing the countryside: (1) very high rural population densities that equal or surpass densities in western suburban areas; (2) large numbers of underemployed workers who could move out of agricultural production without significantly affecting output; (3) historical antecedents in craft traditions; (4) resourceful local leadership; (5) entrepreneurial talents and promotional savvy; and (6) a high level of household savings, a large part of which is used to reinvest in business, with the remainder going to build modern family homes and to improve the physical appearance of towns and villages. In the concluding section, the chapter turns briefly to the innovative practice, now common throughout China, of holding periodic elections for village leadership and the implications for the future of electoral democracy in China.

Closely linked to the story of rural urbanization is the heightened spatial mobility, especially of rural people living in the poorer regions in the interior who were left behind in the sudden rush to riches in the coastal cities.

This is the subject of chapter 4. The story begins with an account of the origins of the *hukou* system of household registration, invented early in the Maoist period as a way to hold back the potential "floods" of migrants to cities such as Guangzhou and Shanghai. So long as the country depended on rationing essential items of consumption (food, oil, fuel), this attempt to place severe restraints on migration worked reasonably well by holding down the size of cities and thus also the costs of urbanization. But as soon as the post-1978 reforms kicked in, the *hukou* system became a serious drag on the economy. More or less free markets in everything except labor turned out to be an unworkable option, and the *hukou* system underwent several modifications, effectively relaxing, though not completely eliminating, official restraints on mobility. In the end, however, tens of millions of migrants left the countryside for the newly urbanizing regions in search of work. Known popularly as "floaters," newcomers were met with disdain by urbanites who were used to their own, more sophisticated ways of living and worried about having to share their privileges with the uncouth masses from the countryside. But villagers were needed as "temporary" workers, so they settled on the outskirts of the city and began to apply their considerable energies and talents to the tasks at hand. Many worked in construction, and young women found work in garment factories and domestic services. Whole families moved into the old farmhouses in the rural-urban fringe to take up back-breaking work in the rice paddies, while the resident villagers took up jobs in newly sprouted factories or simply lived as rentiers, collecting distributions from the collective enterprises of the village and renting out their homes to migrant workers.

Despite a great deal of anecdotal evidence, there is little data on the several dimensions of this massive movement from farm to city. Distinctions have to be made between serial, repeat, cyclical, return, and permanent migrations, and those taking place over short versus long distances. Illegal migrants must be conceptually separated from official migrants, and the very category of "migrant" must be defined with precision. In one of the few well-done statistical surveys, conducted in seven provinces prominent as places of origin of migrants, it turned out that only 3.1 percent of peasant households had members who were absent from their homes for more than one year. Moreover, some of these migrants had moved only to a nearby township rather than to one of the eastern metropolises. Two-thirds of the households had lost no one to the outside world.

Following this analysis, chapter 4 documents some of the dismal conditions of work migrants encounter in their places of destination, and covers the formation of migrant enclaves in Beijing and Shanghai. The chapter concludes by discussing the findings from a single study on the important topic of return migration, and the impact returning migrants have on their home communities.

Chapter 5 looks at some of the ways in which reforms over the past two decades have affected everyday life in cities. The work unit system, which had held all workers captive in walled compounds, provided for their daily needs, but also kept them under constant surveillance and supervision, was abandoned. *Danwei* continued as an organizational form, but they were no longer required to assume responsibility for the lives of their workers from cradle to grave. Some *danwei* simply went bankrupt; others took foreign partners on board and began producing for export, while their greatly reduced work force sought to reinvent their lives in the new economy beyond the walls. Many of the older workers retired, others started small informal enterprises on their own, and some even found work in "rural" industries in the suburbs.

One of the features of life in the newly open (or rather, half-open) cities was people's discovery that they now had responsibility for organizing their own leisure time. For many urban residents, leisure activities took up an increasing portion of their lives. People could now devote themselves to their hobbies (which swept through in waves during the 1980s and 1990s), from ballroom dancing to collecting songbirds and crickets. There was also a sudden outburst of interest in various sorts of spiritual movement, generically called *qigong.* As high-rise apartment buildings soared skyward, new middle-class households could move into the privacy of their own homes, turn on the television set, and relax, leaving behind the world outside their own four walls. They had ceased to be merely workhorses and were on the way to becoming urban consumers. But first they had to become knowledgeable in their new role. The government had a stake in the process, and consumer protection groups soon sprang up that pursued their objective with vigor, helping to bring justice to defrauded clients and to raise overall quality standards.

I have arranged all of these issues under the general heading of "expanding spheres of personal autonomy." While there is no imminent possibility that China's Communist Party will tolerate a challenge to its monopoly of power, various innovative forms of political life are emerging at provincial and local levels, in some instances even with the active encouragement of the party. One such experiment is reported from the newly established province of Hainan, a large island in the south of China. Under the label of "small government, big society," the province appears to be pushing the limits of what a socialist market society can bear. The chapter concludes with a discussion of the problem of a "civil society" in China's cities. Rejecting the notion of a "public sphere" as posited by the German philosopher Jürgen Habermas, I argue that there exists a considerable capacity for self-organization, and that the many new associations that are springing up in China's cities, though nominally supervised by the party-state, constitute an important source of interest articulation.

Local governance is the topic of chapter 6. In one sense, it is a new subject for postrevolutionary China. Under Mao's regime, the city of *danwei* required no complicated governance structures, since central planning cascaded down the command structure from Beijing to the remotest neighborhood and village. But if we look further back, into the history of imperial China, we can gain new perspectives for interpreting the present. For the existing governance system is very much cut from the same cloth as that of the past.

The chapter begins with an examination of the role of the *yamen,* or government office, at county levels as it existed during the late imperial era. Historically, the august presence of the emperor's representative—the magistrate—was symbolized by the walls around the capital city, at the center of which stood the walled government compound. The magistrate's job was to ensure that imperial policies were carried out, but his main task was to send up the prescribed quota of taxes to higher levels and to maintain the public order at home. In principle, his authority extended across the entire county— that is, to all of the emperor's subjects, especially those toiling in the fields beyond the city walls. But in practice, he seldom left the city, leaving it to the unpopular "runners" to collect taxes from village households, line their own pockets and those of their masters, and report any disturbances and rumors of rebellion. His main business in the city was twofold: to dispense local justice and to settle disputes. In other words, the magistrate dealt with local gentry and merchants, which turned out to be a highly remunerative and mutually advantageous business. It is these elites that were the real power in the city, its informal government that maintained the essential public services of the city.

From these imperial beginnings, formal city governments first emerged in the republican interregnum of the 1920s and 1930s, but the chaotic circumstances of the time kept them from consolidating. Instead, the tradition of informal governance by local elites continued, reinforced by the presence of large numbers of uniformed police who took on increasing responsibilities under the mantle of public order. Beijing in the 1920s had the reputation of being the best policed city in the world!

Urban governance during the period of revolutionary communism was a relatively simple matter. Collective life was organized around the *danwei* and was run, at least in theory, like clockwork from commands that filtered down from Beijing through two parallel hierarchies: the Communist Party and the functional ministries under the State Council. With the gradual dismantling of the *danwei* system in the reform era, however, municipal governments were suddenly confronted with a whole range of new responsibilities, which they had to tackle with virtually no resources from the center. The first problem, then, as the central government retreated from local affairs (though without relinquishing its ultimate authority to intervene) was financial: how to raise the necessary cash to do whatever needed to be done for urban progress. Help came from two sides. First, since land is owned collectively, it can be leased, and when new industries, housing, airports, and ports need to be built, the hunger for land is very great. Second, collectively owned and profitable businesses can help defray the cost of public undertakings.

Exploiting these two sources of income, not only for cities, but also for urban districts (boroughs) and Street Offices (neighborhoods)—a terminology left over from the Maoist era—has created a situation that one observer calls "amphibiousness," where the business of government is not only to satisfy the needs of the city for basic services but also to conduct what are hoped to be profitable undertakings. Amphibiousness, alas, also leads to corruption, and while a certain amount of self-serving behavior is generally tolerated, so long as those involved do the proper thing for the community, excesses are strongly resented. As a result, the government has been forced, however reluctantly, to take on some very prominent individuals and dispense such justice as may be warranted: fines, demotions, removal from office, jail, or execution.

Chapter 6 finally turns in some detail to the question of urban planning. Although first ideas on urban planning as a reform movement were published in 1919 by Sun Fo, Sun Yat-sen's younger son who would soon become mayor of Guangzhou (Canton), urban planning languished during Mao's time and was only resurrected in the mid-1980s. Since then it has made rapid strides, with some sixty thousand trained, partially trained, and even untrained planners staffing the offices of cities up and down the China coast. Their mandated job is to prepare master plans for cities large and small and to implement these plans through a system of administrative controls on location, land use, and other requirements. But there are far too many actors in the land development and planning game now, and events move faster than planners can draw up their plans, so their immediate effectiveness is not very great. Still, the profession is consolidating, and ingenious planners find ways of inserting themselves into urban policy questions where their concerns can be heard.

Finally, in the conclusion, I review some of the lessons that can be drawn from the preceding analysis, and raise the question of "sustainable" cities. In addition to the usual triad of economic, ecological, and social sustainability, whose principles may be mutually incompatible, I suggest that the path of transformation itself needs to be "sustainable" in the sense of "steering the middle passage" between the two poles of stasis and chaos. An important aspect of such a path is the value that attaches to continuities with China's own past, its values and institutions. Three strategic issues are then raised under the broad heading of a "sustainable urban development." They include environmental conditions in major cities, focusing on Wuhan and Kunming; the rising specter of unemployment in cities and the terrifying prospect of "jobless growth"; and, finally, the rising levels of poverty and income inequality in cities. Clearly, there is no convenient cutoff point to the story told in these pages, and much will depend on how China's rulers respond to the challenges that lie ahead.

One topic absent from my account, but perhaps of considerable interest to readers beyond China's borders, is the question of whether the urban transition—impelled by the determined drive for rapid economic growth and the opening up of the economy not only to global capital but also, however fitfully, to the circulation of ideas and popular culture—will eventually lead to a political transition as well, away from the party-state of the present to a more pluralist form. In other words, readers might ask whether the transition toward a competitive and relatively open market economy will have a counterpart in the political sphere (Lindau and Cheek 1998).

This question, though compelling, is essentially speculative and not directly related to any of the several dimensions of the urban transition. It is for this reason, for example, that I prefer to speak of "expanding spheres of personal autonomy" in the everyday life of local citizens in contemporary China, rather than of the prospects for democracy. My point of reference is the actually existing China, rather than a China of some hypothetical future. China, as I have emphasized, is one of the world's great civilizations. Culturally, it is not a *tabula rasa* to be colonized by Western conceptions of the good society. As so often observed, even commodity markets function in culturally specific ways in China. In the structural sense, markets are institutionally defined; phenomenologically, they are defined by culturally agreeable ways of doing business. Ultimately, China must be understood on its own terms, viewed, to the extent that it is possible for a foreign observer to do so, from the inside, judged by its own standards rather than by standards that are largely irrelevant to its history. The perspicacious reader will undoubtedly come upon passages in this text where I have failed to live up to this ideal of interpretation, but overall I have tried to abide by it.

Before the Common Era (BCE)

Shang, 1600–ca. 1050
Western Zhou, 1025–256
Spring and Autumn period (formation of first great kingdoms), 722–482
Warring States, 453–221
Jin (the first unified state), 221–206   *Qin*
Western Han, 206 BCE–9 CE

Common Era (CE)

Eastern Han, 25–220
Period of fragmentation ("dark ages"), 220–581   三国二晋南北朝?
Sui (reunification of China), 581–618
Tang, 618–907
Northern Song, 960–1127
Southern Song, 1127–1279
Yuan (Mongol empire), 1271–1367
Ming (restoration of the Mandarin state), 1368–1644
Qing (Manchu empire), 1644–1911
Republic of China, 1912–49
People's Republic of China, **1949–present** (revolutionary communism
    under Mao Zedong, 1949–76; reform period, from 1978)

General chronology of Chinese history

1. Historical Traces

According to Paul Wheatley, a geographer who explored the genesis of Chinese cities, the North China Plain was one of a limited number of regions where cities first developed (Wheatley 1971).[1] Archaeological records, primarily from excavations at Anyang in the lower Wei River valley, suggest that urban settlements first appeared during the late Shang dynasty, or about 1600 BCE, but more reliable information dates from about a thousand years later, during the period of small principalities known as the Western Zhou.

> The mosaic of settlements spread over the North China plain early in the Western Zhou comprised old Shang foundations dating from before the conquest, tribal villages which had existed outside the framework of an organized polity until the advent of the Zhou overlords, and, perhaps most important of all, the garrison establishments of the new dynasty. Each of these settlement forms was integrated into the political structure of the Zhou kingdom, and each sooner or later, despite its distinctive origins, assumed a role in the emergence of a hierarchy of cities, each unit of which at each level of the system combined ceremonial, military, and agricultural functions. At the apex of the hierarchy was the imperial city of G'og in the Wei valley, the style center whence diffused the intellectual, religious, social, and aesthetic values of Western Zhou culture. (Wheatley 1971, 173–74)

According to Chinese beliefs, the Zhou city, and especially the royal capital, had to be properly aligned with the spiritual forces of Heaven. Thus, "one of the . . . essential features of the Western Zhou city, at whichever level of the hierarchy it occurred, was the altar to the god of the soil which . . . was always kept open to receive the hoar frost, dew, wind, and rain and to allow free access by the influences of Heaven and Earth. The roofing-over of this altar signified the extinction both of the ruler's line and of the state and the city. The state might subsequently be reconstituted and the city rebuilt or resuscitated, but for the time being, both were extinguished" (175). The altar to the god of the soil served as the symbol of the continuing power of the state. Two additional sacred symbols, particularly in regard to dynastic capitals, deserve mention: the ancestral temple, which contained the tablets of the former rulers of the realm whose spirits had to be propitiated, and the Altar of Heaven, which was typically placed just outside the city walls. Heaven ruled human affairs and invested power in legitimate overlords. This was called the Mandate of Heaven. The mandate, however, could be withdrawn, bringing ruin to the kingdom (Wright 1977, 39–41).

By the Age of the Warring States, just before the creation of the first empire under the Jin, royal capitals were no longer solely seats of divinely ordained political power. In the words of Jacques Gernet (1996, 72), "they tended to become big commercial and manufacturing centres, and the most recent excavations have disclosed that their walls were enlarged at the end of the age of the Warring States. . . . In fact, the object of the wars in the third century was often the conquest of these big commercial centres." These quarreling kingdoms were finally subdued by the powerful but short-lived Jin dynasty. With its anti-Confucian ideology and legalistic concept of order, the Jin was a brutal, militarist regime. It conquered the several kingdoms that had been fighting each other for generations and created a central state. By erecting the Great Wall, the Jin rulers attempted to secure the agricultural settlements of China against the constant threat of incursions by nomadic "barbarians" from the northern steppes. The regime's greatest success was the political unification of China, but its turbulent life was brief, and its successor dynasty, the Western Han, replaced Jin militarism with a Confucian ideology.[2]

Literati schooled in the classics and attached to the emperor's court reconstructed the principles that supposedly had governed city-building during the Zhou and set them out as the template for their own and future generations. The imperial capital was thus conceived as the "pivot of the four quarters," that is, of All under Heaven, signifying benevolent imperial rule. City walls surrounding hierarchically ordered administrative centers were to be raised not for security's sake alone but also to symbolize the august presence of imperial authority throughout the realm. The siting of any new city was determined by conducting the proper auguries that would ensure its alignment with benign cosmic forces that would generate peace and prosperity.[3]

THE ARISTOCRATIC EMPIRE OF THE
SUI AND TANG DYNASTIES

The fall of the Eastern Han in 220 CE was followed by centuries of disunity—China's "dark ages"—which ended only with the establishment of the Sui dynasty, another of the great unifiers in Chinese history. The Han had built their capital, Chang'an, in their northern power base, the region called "the land within the passes," a well-watered and fertile plain surrounded by mountains. Eight hundred years later, Chang'an seemed a small, shabby city, unfit for the victorious emperor Yang Jian, who wished to proclaim his rule in a far more resplendent capital city. And so he began the construction of the new City of Everlasting Peace, named Chang'an like the capital of his Han predecessors who had once ruled over a unified China.[4] The Sui dynasty did not last long, but the newly ascendant rulers of the Tang continued the embellishment of their city, which was eventually to house over a million people.

Tang Chang'an was a city of walls. Its outer perimeter of rammed earth measured 37 km, and visitors entered the city through one of its many gates, at least some of which were surmounted by imposing gate towers. Within this fortified perimeter, the walled palace city was located to the north. Aristocrats and commoners alike lived in walled *fang*, or wards, that were separated by wide avenues. The enormous expanse of the so-called Heavenly Road, measuring 150–155 m across, provided the central axis that linked the imperial complexes to the Gate of Luminous Virtue to the south, one of the four cardinal gates of the city. Like all roads in Chang'an, it was made of compacted earth and was lined with trees (Heng 1999). An eastern and a western market, both walled, were the end points of major transcontinental trading routes.

To live in Chang'an was to live in a highly regimented city. Heng Chye Kiang provides a vivid account.

> The population of Chang'an lived in . . . walled wards which were closed off at night by the ward headman who kept the keys of the gates and was also responsible for maintaining law and order within the wards after nightfall. . . . Unless a permit was issued by the county officials or the ward headman's office as in the case of an emergency, illness or marriage, no one was allowed out in the avenues at night. . . . At the corners of the wards, i.e., the junction of the avenues, were guard posts manned by detachments of the Jinwu Guard. Depending on the size of the post, 5 or 30 might be stationed [there]. [Few] activities went on within the

Chang'an and its "Six Streets"

wards in the evening. A poem written by Quan Deyu has a line that says "A thousand doors were quiet when the ward gates were opened or closed." (1999, 23–24)

Beginning in the winter of 636, drums were set up in the six major avenues to announce the opening and closing of the ward gates. According to the treatise on officials in the New History of T'ang: "At sunset, the drums were beaten 800 times and the gates were closed. From the second night watch, mounted soldiers employed by the officers in charge of policing the streets made the rounds in silence. At the fifth watch, the drums in all the streets were beaten so as to let the noise be heard everywhere; then all the gates of the wards and markets were opened." The morning drums must have been very important in the daily rhythm of the city since they were beaten 300 times before the opening of the gates. Before 636, instead of drumbeats, military patrols shouted the signal in the streets (ibid.).

As the Tang regime went into decline, the rigid order of its cities crumbled, and a new kind of city gradually took shape. Heng Chye Kiang calls it an "open city" and evokes it with the example of Kaifeng, capital of the Northern Song at the beginning of the twelfth century, shortly before the city was sacked by the invading Mongols (Heng 1999, chap. 4):

> The emergence . . . of the open city announced the advent of a very different form of city. The new urban center was crisscrossed by streets lined with establishments of all kinds including shops, taverns, restaurants, ateliers, entertainment facilities, religious institutions, government edifices, and residences. Extensive suburbs often mushroomed outside the city walls. Within, overpopulation and high density forced buildings to be built closely together. Multistory buildings became common. Free to move, shops and entertainment facilities congregated at bridges and important intersections of major land and water routes both inside and outside the city walls, creating busy commercial districts. Business was conducted at all hours of the day [or night]. (205–6)

Though resplendent in scale, Chang'an had still very much the look of a fortified military camp. Commerce, despised by the court, was ranked below peasant farming, and was strictly supervised. With the Song dynasty, however, the imperial house came once more under the growing influence of the scholar-bureaucrats whose dominance would continue, with interruptions, until the collapse of the Qing dynasty and the proclamation of the republic on January 1, 1912. As Heng observes,

> The strong, autocratic grip that the Sui emperors had over their capitals was replaced by that of a bureaucratic government of practical scholar-officials. Trade once strictly regulated in enclosed markets and conducted primarily for the court's consumption was widespread and permeated all levels of society. Under the Song administration, commercial and urban taxes became major sources of income for the court. The slackening of commercial controls went hand in hand with the relaxation of urban regulations. Street encroaching structures were

Street scene in Kaifeng, capital of the Northern Song

taxed but accepted. The rationalism of the Song reign turned an urban problem into a money-making opportunity and accepted the birth of a new urban structure (1999, 207).[5]

THE LATE IMPERIAL ERA

Throughout China's imperial age, a city was an urban settlement that had been designated as an administrative seat of the central government. To signify the government presence, such cities were typically enclosed by walls of impressive proportions.[6] In addition to the dynastic capital, there were provincial, prefectural, and county tiers of territorial administration.[7] But inevitably, as the empire and its population grew, the ability of the imperial court to effectively govern the country from its urban bases down to the mundane level of everyday life declined. William Skinner was the first scholar to draw attention to the fact that despite huge increases in territory and population, the number of counties into which China was divided had remained roughly the same over a period of nearly two thousand years, fluctuating between 1,200 and 1,500 *xian* (1977, 21). The enlarged territories of the counties, their large populations, and the difficulties and hardships of travel meant that imperial officials lacked effective means to direct local affairs, which remained largely, if informally, self-administered.[8] From the Tang dynasty onward, Skinner extrapolates a steady decline in imperial power to intervene effectively in local affairs.

At the village level, clan or lineage associations were the leading force for order. In urban settlements, local elites, organized into federations of trade, craft, temple, neighborhood, and native place associations, provided the necessary arrangements for governance, including dispute resolution, policing, charity work, public health, the construction and/or maintenance of urban infrastructure, outfitting of a militia in turbulent times, and more. From the Song dynasty onward, and particularly during later periods, local civil society was well organized and ready to shoulder the responsibilities for the general welfare. Except for major public works and onerous tax farming, the imperial government left both cities and countryside largely to their own devices. It was a government of benign neglect.[9]

Of particular interest are the various civic associations of urban sojourners organized on the basis of their place of native origin. Throughout the late imperial era, from Ming to Qing, temporary migrants made up well over half the population of most cities. Although many of those who came to the city stayed on, they retained a connection to their place of birth or (more remotely) ancestral origin. According to Skinner, "the normative pattern was clear: a young man who left to seek his fortune was expected to return home for marriage, to spend there an extended period of mourning on the death of either parent, and eventually to retire in the locality where his ancestors were buried. Even when these expectations were not realized, the son born to a sojourner inherited his father's native place along with his surname. . . . [W]ithin the span of a few generations native place must be seen as an ascribed characteristic" (1977d, 539). Migration was primarily a male prerogative, and sons were selected by their families to make a career away from home in the hope that they would bring fortune and glory to the family left behind. Within cities, the male to female ratio was thus exceptionally high (up to more than 250 men per 100 women in Hankou). The distinction between sojourners and residents, coupled with urban residents' negative attitudes towards temporary migrants (popularly known as "floaters" in contemporary China), has carried forward to the present time, and underlies whatever legitimacy still resides in the residence permit (*hukou*) system, of which more later. Even when they came from nearby places, sojourners were usually regarded as "ethnic" Others who were not entitled to their full rights as citizens (ibid., 544). Though in some general sense they might all be Han, their "unintelligible" dialect and unfamiliar customs marked them as "inferior."

As for the intellectual elites, their places of permanent residence were typically dispersed throughout the realm. But if engaged in public affairs, they would spend many years of their active life in cities. Upon their retirement, they would often return to the market towns, gentry estates, or ancestral villages. This phenomenon led Frederick Mote to argue that for most of China's history, there was little to distinguish urban from rural culture. "The rural component of Chinese civilization was more or less uniform, and it extended everywhere that Chinese civilization penetrated. It, and not the cities, defined the Chinese way of life. It was like the net in which the cities and towns of China were suspended. . . . To extend this metaphor, China's cities were but knots of the same material, of one piece with the net, denser in quality but not foreign bodies resting on it" (1977, 105). Mote speaks of a rural/urban continuum as typical for China, though *interweaving* might be a better term for it.[10] In any event, by the beginning of the twentieth century, only about 6 percent of the country's population lived in urban agglomerations of fifty thousand or more population (Elvin 1974, 3). In what ways even this population could be called urban in a deeper sociological sense must, at least for the time being, remain unanswered.

Urban identities began to form toward the end of the imperial era. In his exemplary history of nineteenth-century Hankou, William T. Rowe (1989) suggests a growing self-awareness on the part of China's urban population.[11]

> No less than in the post-medieval West, a distinctive urban culture and mentality had come to characterize the largest cities of late imperial China. City-dwellers were quite aware of their distinctiveness, even though Chinese urban culture probably did share more elements with rural traditions than did its counterpart in Europe, and Confucian pastoral ideals worked to soften the sense of self-conscious urban superiority so evident in the West. In China as in Europe the greater intensity and diversity of communications media helped differentiate urban from rural life, and in both civilizations the early modern proliferation of literacy and of written media, joining older oral and visual forms, was very largely an urban phenomenon. (62)

This increasingly urban orientation on the part of the urban gentry and commercial elites took concrete form in the provision of what Rowe calls community institutions.[12] Rowe even claims that there existed an "articulated public sphere," most notably in cities (10).[13] During the latter half of the nineteenth century, as the Qing dynasty was losing its grip on power, the countryside was in upheaval. Banditry and piracy were on the rise, rural famine was widespread, and landless laborers ("vagrants") drifted into the city. Among the vagrants, the men worked for minimal wages as nightwatchmen or became beggars and thieves, and women sold their bodies for sex. Especially after the devastating Taiping Rebellion (1850–64), the city was becoming a refuge from the impoverished countryside. In response to this situation, the imperial government ordered the reinstitution of the *bao jia* surveillance system in Hankou. But like all previous attempts to revive this unpopular system of social control, the effort ended in failure.[14]

As a major inland city, nineteenth-century Hankou remained relatively untouched by the dramatic events that were engulfing coastal cities at the time, when first British and soon other European and Asian powers (Japan, Russia) forced the opening of China to foreign trade on their own terms. The first Opium War resulted in the famous Treaty of Nanjing in 1842, when China was forced to yield Hong Kong to the British Crown and to open five port cities—Guangzhou, Xiamen, Fuzhou, Ningbo, and Shanghai—to European settlement under conditions of extra-territorial status. Thus began what Gernet (1996, 581) calls China's encirclement. Seventy years later, the number of so-called treaty ports had grown to thirty-two, ranging from Harbin in the north to Kunming in the south. The "crown jewel" in this array of cities, however, was Shanghai, which would become not only China's most industrialized city but also its most cosmopolitan. As Shanghai went, so went the nation. All eyes would soon be on the budding metropolis on the muddy Huangpu River to learn from its experience, to imitate its fashions, as the city became the center of China's slow awakening to modernity (Wasserstrom 1999).

Internal weaknesses, military defeats, and lack of vision all contributed to the final collapse of China's dynastic period. By the end of 1911, the empire was no more. But the republic that was proclaimed was unable to govern effectively. For the next thirty-eight years, the increasingly fragmented territory of China became a battleground among competing warlords. In 1931 Japanese armies invaded Manchuria, where they installed a puppet Manchu emperor before marching south and conquering much of China, including Shanghai and the ancient southern capital of Nanjing. Communist insurgents under Mao Zedong fought against both the nominal nationalist government led by Chiang Kai-shek and the foreign invaders. Amid all this turmoil, daily life in urban China struggled on, not least because of the strength of urban civil society and the informal institutions of governance that had already been a notable feature of life in nineteenth-century Hankou. A particularly vivid account of the struggles to maintain something like normal life in a rapidly modernizing Beijing during the 1920s is David Strand's *Rickshaw Beijing*, which focuses on the informal politics of the city (Strand 1989). Whole-city studies, such as those of Rowe and Strand, have given us the empirical grounding for understanding the broader historical forces that were relentlessly pushing China into the modern age.[15]

THE UNIFICATION OF CHINA UNDER REVOLUTIONARY COMMUNISM

The People's Republic of China (PRC) was proclaimed in 1949. China was once again unified, with Beijing as its capital, but the country's borders were soon closed against the outside world. In a country of peasants, the revolution could be said to have been led by peasants. Once order was restored, however, the new regime set out on a course of centrally planned, "forced march" industrialization. China would not "develop," as that concept was conventionally understood in the capitalist world. Money would not be the primary medium of exchange as it is in a market economy. Planning would be done, Soviet-style, through a system of "material balances." Basic needs would be collectively provided. Cities would be transformed into engines of production, rather than remain as sites of decadent consumption. And because all this would be done without foreign investments, it would require a high internal rate of savings, a rate that, in a country that was mostly rural, would have to be squeezed out of the agricultural sector.

This imperative accounted for many of the new regime's policies. The rural commune system instituted in the late 1950s allowed resources to be transferred to urban-based industrialization. And urbanization, particularly in the largest cities, would be restrained, with social infrastructure held to the barest minimum. Large-scale industries, along with other state-operated institutions, such as universities, were organized as work units (*danwei*), which in some ways were like miniature walled cities structured around production. Finally, the potential flow of rural labor to cities was to be tightly regulated.

A quick summary of changes in the levels of urbanization from 1949 onward may help us see what actually took place and how it was accomplished.[16] The early years of the PRC saw a huge influx of population into cities. The urbanized portion of the total population nearly doubled between 1949 and 1960, leaping from 10.1 percent to 19.7 percent. In 1960 131 million people were registered as living in cities. This was followed by a stressful period of de-urbanization, which stabilized at around 17.3 percent urban in the early 1970s. In absolute numbers, however, urban population would continue to grow. At the beginning of the reform era in 1982, the number of people residing in 239 cities and 2,819 officially designated towns stood at 215 million (21.1 percent) and would continue to increase rapidly thereafter.[17]

Kam Wing Chan (1994) provides a succinct summary of major policy initiatives that helped to restrain the urbanization process and to hold down its costs in the interest of maximizing the expansion of industrial production.

1. A household registration (*hukou*) system was instituted in 1960 that fixed a person's residence to his or her native place. In addition, a person's *hukou* identity was divided into agricultural and nonagricultural so that, in principle, he or she could work in the city as a contract agricultural laborer or in the countryside as a nonagricultural cadre. In either case, the *hukou* was a card of entitlement. Nonagricultural *hukou* holders were entitled to subsidized grains, housing, and education, privileges not enjoyed by holders of agricultural *hukou*, who were supposedly self-supporting. In a society where labor was allocated by the state (there was no labor market) and where basic commodities (food, lodging, consumer

products) were rationed, and coupons could only be redeemed in one's place of permanent residence, the *hukou* system was an effective means to prevent urban-bound migration.[18] It also created a two-class society of privileged urban residents and second-class rural citizens. A common expression of the time put it wryly: migration to cities was like "climbing to heaven" (ibid., 77).[19]

2. Even so, most industrial jobs (and they were expanding rapidly) were located in cities. To meet the resulting problem of labor shortages, state-owned enterprises were permitted to enter into labor contracts with agricultural communes to recruit temporary workers. Lacking urban entitlements, the workers were expected to return to their native places at the end of their contract. Nevertheless, many were able to prolong their stay with the connivance of industrial managers who "hoarded" temporary workers with rural *hukou* and were thus required to make only limited collective provisioning for them (housing, child care, and so forth).

3. Beginning in 1957 and continuing through the decade of the Cultural Revolution, attempts were made to ship out millions of urbanites to the countryside. Some of them were unemployed or social undesirables (e.g., vagrants, intellectuals, and those with landlord ancestries). Others were middle-school and high-school graduates for whom there were no suitable jobs in the city and who were sent into the countryside to help teach peasants the rudiments of reading and writing—and, in turn, to learn from them about the harsh life in China's rural backlands. During the early 1960s more than 20 million urban residents were returned to the countryside for economic reasons. Another 30 million were "rusticated" during the decade of the Cultural Revolution from 1966 to 1976 (ibid., 78).[20]

4. One way to avoid urbanization costs and, at the same time, to raise rural incomes was to encourage the establishment of industries in nonurban areas under the collective management of communes and brigades (townships). This was a very popular program, and by 1978 about 28 percent (17 million) of China's total industrial labor force was working in collectively managed rural industries. During the Maoist era, all employees in the commune- and brigade-run industry sector were classified in the national income accounts as "agricultural" and were thus ineligible for urban entitlements (ibid., 81).[21]

5. New housing construction was held to an absolute minimum. A survey of 192 cities discovered that between 1950 and 1978, per-capita floor area had

declined from 4.5 m² to 3.6 m², a drop of 20 percent (ibid., 73). Besides, the quality of construction was generally shoddy, and maintenance was poor.

6. Urban population was also held in check by the one-child-per-family policy that was first introduced in urban areas during the early 1960s and later promoted in the countryside as well, except for ethnic "autonomous" regions. "The result," writes Chan, "no doubt aided greatly by the drastic rise in women's labour participation and the deteriorating urban housing conditions, is significant. The total urban fertility rate declined from about five to six in the mid-1950s and early 1960s to an impressive level of 1.5 in the mid-1970s and onward" (ibid., 80).

So what did the new socialist city, subject to all of these policies, look like? We have already seen the numbers. Contrary to experiences in other industrializing countries—all of them market economies—Maoist China achieved a sevenfold increase in the net material product of industry per unit of urban population (ibid., 83). But at the same time, cities also acquired a new look. Here is how Piper Rae Gaubatz (1995) describes them:

The multifunctional compounds built by Chinese work units since 1949 are walled areas somewhat reminiscent of the walled wards of the early traditional Chinese city. . . . [T]he work-unit compound became a miniature city within its own walls, offering residents spaces for work and for play, for home life and for neighborhood life. The highly controlled environment of the work-unit compound is entered through a guarded gate. . . . Within the gate, the architecture is utilitarian and regimented. Production facilities and residential facilities are usually housed in separate structures. Orderly rows of residential structures commonly consist of three- to five-story brick or cement buildings. . . . Common areas between the buildings . . . serve as bicycle parking lots, children's play areas, recreation places for volley ball and other sports, and green areas. Other facilities within the walled compound vary but ideally include dining halls, provision shops, medical facilities, recreation facilities, meeting rooms, and administrative offices. Thus the work-unit compound serves as the locus for organization of many facets of life. . . .

Neighborhood committees sometimes also functioned as work-units. By organizing small production workshops and other neighborhood labor they limited the need for long-distance mobility within the city. . . .

Thus ideals of social and spatial organization were creating distinctly undifferentiated social and functional landscapes. . . . Coupled with preferences for

Academic work unit (*danwei*) housing and high school campus, Beijing, mid-1990s

low-cost, low-rise structures, this resulted in the development of an urban environment with three prominent characteristics: generalized functional organization, low-rise standardized landscapes, and the persistence of the "walking-scale" of the city. (29–32)

To this description of the Maoist city, an ideal that for a variety of reasons was never fully realized, one is tempted to add a final observation. The Maoist regime was intent on turning "capitalist" cities—that is, cities geared to consumption—into cities of production. Cities were thus essentially machines for maximizing output that would be centrally managed by an official cadre. Nearly every able-bodied person worked (urban labor force participation reached an extraordinary 82 percent), and even leisure activities were, for the most part, collectively organized. As a result, civil society, which had been quite active during the republican period and, as we have seen, even during the Qing dynasty, had no chance of flourishing. Where it broke through the cracks in the pavement, it was vigorously, and often viciously, suppressed. In ways that would have been inconceivable during the imperial era, China's citizenry, having only recently emerged from dynastic rule, were reduced to being passive subjects of the state. Under these conditions, an autonomous civic life was inconceivable.[22]

After Mao's death in 1976, the struggle for succession lasted three years, ending with the supremacy of Deng Xiaoping. The following decades came to be known as the reform period. As China opened its borders to the outside world and gradually introduced a market economy, life began to change dramatically. At the same time, Western scholars—anthropologists, sociologists, historians, geographers, sinologists, political scientists, and others— started to arrive in droves to observe what was happening in the former Middle Kingdom. In the following chapters I will selectively and critically assess some of this literature in order to provide a synthetic sketch of China's urban transition.

THE VIEW FROM THE CITY

Until quite recently, it was common to picture China as a rural society in which the distinctive life of cities could be safely ignored or, more accurately, in which city life was essentially conflated with life in the countryside (Mote 1977; Faure and Liu 2002). This historiography has changed to the extent that there is now a burgeoning English-language literature concerned with urban life. Much of the credit for this must go to the pioneering work of

G. William Skinner, whose collective volume *The City in Late Imperial China* remains a landmark of scholarship (Skinner, ed., 1977). The endpapers of his volume show the cities of China in 1894. They depict a dense pattern of urban places, as if to provoke the question of how our views of China would change if we looked at the country from the vantage point of this dense network of the urban. In the case of Europe, we are accustomed to an urban-based interpretation of history as far back as classical Greece. And yet, as Jacques Gernet reminds us, as late as 1830, less than 20 percent of the population of Europe lived in towns. The Europe of that period was still a region of peasant farmers, and only slightly more urban than China itself (Gernet 1996, 544). And yet, our focus even then was on its cities (Braudel 1992).

Such a shift in perspective to the urban is, I believe, more than a case of "the glass is half full or half empty." It is not enough to see China through the lens of dynastic histories, in which cities appear only incidentally, and then only as imperial capitals. We should also endeavor to see its physical spaces as a kind of double helix of urban hierarchies. One strand is political, moving in descending order from the imperial capital down to the 1500 or so county seats; the other is economic, descending from major trading centers along major long-distance land and sea routes to regional and local markets. These two hierarchies partly overlap, but historically, we can find major trading cities, such as Hankou, that were not administrative centers, and administrative centers whose political importance overshadowed their economic role as trading cities.

In the following chapter, I refer to late imperial China as an archipelago of regions. This seems a reasonable geography for a preindustrial society whose major arteries were rivers and canals. But for much of its long history, China was a politically integrated empire, and the majestic walls of its cities reminded people of the government's presence. In times of flood or political turmoil, people from the surrounding countryside would seek refuge within these sheltering walls. In more peaceful times, they would come to the city to trade. Eventually, some cities emerged as major commercial hubs, linking regions to other regions and to the larger world outside.

The historical glimpses of urban China in the present chapter are meant to alert readers to the possibility that we might reimagine China's history as an urban-based history. As David Strand has observed, "at the end of the twentieth century, [events] have restored the place of urban life at the center of things. . . . One might even argue that the Maoist regime, for all of its pro-village, anti-city rhetoric was fundamentally urban after all" (Strand 1999, 223).

This reassessment need neither denigrate nor deny village China, its customs and traditions, its social movements, its role in making cities possible in the first place. We should rather learn to see rural and urban as being mutually constitutive. Frederick Mote's argument that the culture of cities in China was historically not very different from the culture of the surrounding countryside may well be accurate, but it overlooks the political and economic roles of cities both in controlling rural life and in creating the reality of a Chinese empire whose agents resided in cities. Both the political and economic spaces of China's vast territory were a product of this rural/urban dynamic.

2. Regional Policies

China's urban system can be properly understood only in its regional context. This was one of William Skinner's many brilliant insights into the history of urban China. He saw China as an archipelago whose regions were only loosely connected to each other. "Fairly early in my research on Chinese cities," he writes,

> it became clear that in late imperial times [the regions] formed not a single integrated urban system but several regional systems, each one tenuously connected with its neighbours. In tracing out the overlapping hinterlands of the cities in each one of these regional systems, I came to the realization that the region they jointly defined coincided with minor exceptions to a physiographic unit. In short, it appears that each system of cities developed within a physiographic region. I eventually came to conceive of urban development . . . as a critical element in regional development—the processes whereby regional resources of all kinds, social and cultural as well as economic and political, were multiplied, deployed with greater effectiveness, and exploited with increased efficiency. (1977b, 211)

In his monumental study Skinner identified nine macro-regions, based primarily on a delineation of watersheds. But the real obstacle to interregional commerce was not the physical boundaries of these regions (rivers, mountains, deserts) but the high costs of transaction that gave the subsystem of cities central to each region a set of overlapping hinterlands that defined their periphery, or effective market range.

> Transactions between the centrally located cities of one region and those of another were minimized by the high cost of unmechanized transport and the great distances involved. It cost as much to transport grain 200 miles on the

> back of a pack animal as it did to produce it in the first place, and the corre-
> sponding figure for coal was less than 25 miles. Transport costs of this order
> of magnitude effectively eliminated low-priced bulky goods from interregional
> trade. . . . It should be emphasized that systematic differences in transport
> efficiency affected politico-administrative and social transactions no less than
> commerce: interregional intercourse was depressed in all spheres. (1977b, 217)

This regional character of urban China, based on the physical characteristics of landscape and their economic implications, was reinforced by
cultural factors of ethnicity, language, and history. Over the centuries, the
empire had succeeded in welding the regions into a single, hierarchically
structured state system that lasted well into the twentieth century. Although
from time to time the empire fell apart into warring states, unity was always
reestablished in the end. After the collapse of the Qing, it took nearly four
decades for China to be reunified once more. Today, China's space economy
is gradually becoming more integrated, as the massive construction of highways, new rail lines, airports, and systems of electronic communication links
up its remotest parts. Still, regionalism continues to be an active force in
shaping the country's politics (Rong et al. 1997).

In the following pages, I will discuss the role of regional policy during
the reform era and some of its outcomes. First, however, a backward glance
at regional policy under Maoism provides necessary background.

THE "THIRD FRONT" STRATEGY

Strictly speaking, the Maoist regime of revolutionary communism never
adopted a regional policy in the conventional sense.[1] Although, as mentioned
in chapter 1, the regime attempted to block rural migration to cities, its main
policies were aimed at strengthening a unified China through industrialization—especially through the development of heavy industry—and constructing an egalitarian society conforming to Mao's utopian vision. The project
was not "achieving development," as that term is generally understood, with
its emphasis on economic growth and distributional issues, but "building a
socialist society." Moreover, military considerations were never far from the
surface and were of more immediate concern. There was fear of nuclear war-
fare and attacks from abroad, especially from the United States, and the per-
sisting threat of an invasion by the defeated Guomintang regime that had
entrenched itself on Taiwan and continued to regard itself as China's legitimate ruler. These fears provided the rationale for the so-called Third Front

strategy that would "hide" essential industries in China's western regions. After the Sino-Soviet split in 1960, a new threat loomed along China's long border with the Soviet Union. Defense Minister Lin Biao put it plainly when he urged the building of industries "in the mountains, in dispersion, and in caves" (Yang 1997, 19; Wei 2000, 133–37). Between 1966 and 1970, this centrally directed effort pushed the interior's share of total state investments to over 70 percent. Despite the upheavals of the Cultural Revolution and the major inefficiencies in the implementation of what was essentially a defensive strategy, Third Front construction continued well into the 1970s.

During the decades of Mao's rule, China could still be correctly described as a loose collection of regionalized economies. In line with this geographical fact, and as part of the country's defensive posture, the policy was to promote regional self-reliance in grains and other basic goods. If China could go it alone, so could each of its regions. In size of population, the various regions equaled or exceeded even the largest European countries. While regional self-reliance might save on transport infrastructure, it would also lead to a great deal of duplication in production. But for revolutionary communism, efficiency was never a chief concern. To the extent that Mao Zedong had a regional policy at all, it was primarily for reasons other than efficiency or regional equity.

THE LADDER-STEP DOCTRINE:
LET SOME GET RICH FIRST

With the onset of the reformist regime in 1978, all of these policies were effectively reversed. Instead, the government opted for a "get rich first" policy that privileged coastal cities. The Seventh Five-Year Plan (1986–90) stated that the objective of regional development was to "speed up the development of the coastal region, to put the emphasis on energy and raw materials construction in the central region, and to actively make preparation for the further development of the western region" (Yang 1997, 29). Thus, like Caesar's Gaul, and following provincial boundaries, China was divided into three parts. Based on this rough regionalization, the new Ladder-Step Doctrine was hotly contested. Similar, mostly academic arguments about regional strategy had flourished in Western countries during the 1960s. Should initial advantage be reinforced, or should the aim be a spatially balanced development? In both cases, the question was resolved in favor of initial advantage, in hopes that growth impulses would somehow diffuse outward from initial "core regions" or major growth centers to their respective peripheries (Friedmann

and Weaver 1979, pt. 2). With China moving steadily toward a socialist market economy, other Maoist policies were scrapped as well, not least the policy of regional self-reliance. With China's prospective entry into the World
Trade Organization, productive efficiency was becoming the new watchword
(though in practice it would have to be balanced against an employment
objective), and the general push was toward a more integrated national spatial economy based on regional interdependencies.[2]

A key policy shift under Deng was the opening of China to foreign investments. Agriculture would no longer be the principal source of national savings.
But initially, at least, foreign capital would have to be lured to China, and this
led to the designation of a large number of potential "growth points," at first
along the coast but before long covering most of the country. Reflecting carefully graded autonomies granted by the State Council, they came in various
guises, including open economic areas (e.g., the Pearl River delta), special
economic zones (e.g., Shenzhen), free trade zones, economic and technical
development zones, coastal open cities, river valley open cities, border region

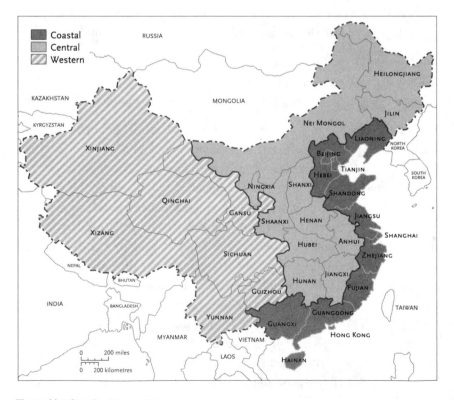

The Ladder-Step Doctrine, 1986

open areas, open provincial capitals, high-technology and new-technology industrial development zones, and state tourist zones, for a total of 424 such focal points (Yang 1997, table 2.4). In addition, three municipalities were raised to provincial status to be directly administered by the State Council: Beijing, Shanghai, and Tianjin. (Subsequently, a greatly expanded municipality of Chongqing was added as a fourth centrally administered city to serve as the economic "growth pole" for Sichuan Province.) This central dispensation of special privileges has created a new competitive environment throughout China (Wei 2000, chapter 3). As for the central government, it could devolve carefully tailored autonomies to provinces, cities, towns, and villages, and also undertook a few major construction projects of its own, such as the Three Gorges Dam. Otherwise, there was little it could do to "steer" the incoming flows of capital. As Khan and Riskin observe (2001, 148), with the progressive decentralization of China's fiscal system, Beijing's budgetary resources as a proportion of GDP are among the lowest in the world. The country's development would have to depend largely on the ingenuity of its local leaders and entrepreneurs (L. White 1998a). State Council policies were for the most part conceived as broad guidelines for local development.

As expected, the implementation of the so-called Ladder-Step Doctrine led to immense changes in the spatial pattern of economic growth. Some parts of the coastal region did indeed make spectacular progress, especially in the Pearl and Yangzi River deltas, the two new "core regions" of China's reform economy. But if almost everyone gained to some extent, they did not all gain at the same pace. The central government was being bombarded with demands for special treatment by just about every province at the same time that many other changes were taking place, driven by market reforms, such as the restructuring and/or closure of state-owned enterprises resulting in massive lay-offs. Consequently, there was a good deal of talk about growing social unrest. The Ninth Five-Year Plan (1996–2000) was already beginning to hint at the need to pay more attention to the central and western regions and to combat poverty in rural areas (Fan 1997, 631; Yang 1997, 95–97). As the millennium year approached, a ladder-step shift to the interior was being signaled.[3]

INKING THE REGIONS:
OWARD AN INTEGRATED NATIONAL MARKET

In some ways, this shift in attention to the central and western regions reflects China's growing integration through massive projects in transport and communication. Slowly but surely, the archipelago of regions is being broken

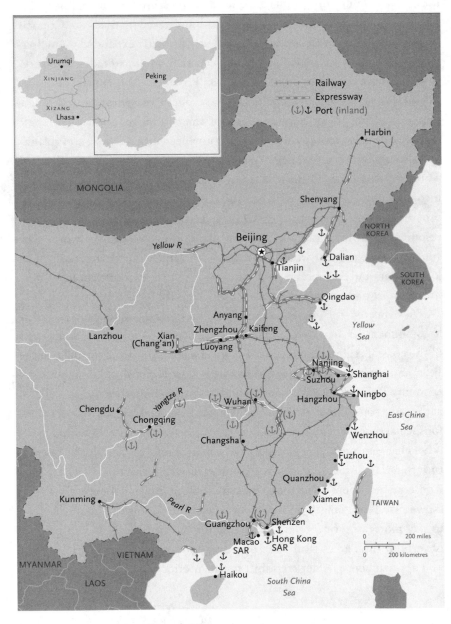

Major transportation nets in China, c. 2000

down. A short, comprehensive account of infrastructure projects can be found in Godfrey Linge's excellent volume on China's new spatial economy (Linge 1997).[4] In an essay entitled "Linking the Regions," Rong Chao-he and his colleagues provide an overview of the enormous challenge of developing an efficient national transport and communication system (Rong et al. 1997). The authors begin their analysis with a bow to Skinner's macro-regions:

> China's space economy consists of a set of loosely articulated functional macro-regions. Overlaid on these is a series of linkages most notably the very large north-south flows of coal, oil, and grain; the east-west flows of raw materials and manufactures (including imports and exports); and the movement, especially of people, between rural and urban areas. . . . Improvements in communications have led to greater spatial interaction, while the development of air travel has enabled more of its citizens to experience the diversity and complexity of their country. (46)

A few examples of infrastructure development and their impact on spatial integration demonstrate the Herculean efforts required. Here, for example, is what Rong and colleagues say about fiber-optic networks and communication satellites:

> The expansion of the fiber-optic network was made a national priority in the early 1990s, and by mid-1994 45,800 km of cable were in place, with the PLA (People's Liberation Army) assisting the Ministry of Posts and Telecommunications (MPT) to roll out some 8,000 km annually to create a system of twenty-two national trunk lines connecting all provincial capitals. The MPT has indicated that a further sixteen national trunk lines will be installed by 2000. . . . China is rolling out about twice as much fibre-optic cabling each year as the United States. (55)

Since 1983, satellites have been used for transmitting national and provincial television programs within China. The use of Mandarin for national news and other broadcasts is gradually helping to break down some of the long-standing language, ethnic, and other barriers across the country (57).

But the biggest challenge in developing an effective national market is ground transportation. In the late 1980s the central government announced its plan to construct the National Trunk Highway System, a network of more than 36,000 km of high-speed highways that would ultimately connect all cities with populations of more than 1 million and 98 percent of those cities with populations between 500,000 and 1 million (Ho and Lin 2004, 93). By the end of 2000 this national road system was half-completed. China's railway capacity also continues to be seriously inadequate, in part because priority in shipments is given to coal, building materials, and other bulk freight. As Rong and his colleagues point out:

> Space for non-priority freight has to be booked weeks in advance and there is no certainty as to when consignments will reach their destination, thus tying up capital in stock-in-transit and making "just-in-time" manufacturing strategies impossible. About one-third of the hubs in the network are saturated; the number of serious "bottle-necks" has doubled since the early 1980s; and the lack of places where trains can pass further constrains operations.
>
> In general, roads are poorly maintained, with vehicular traffic having to share narrow pavements with pedestrians, bicycles, donkey carts, and tractors. Although 90 per cent of the 1.2 million km of roads are described as "paved," only about 4 per cent can handle even 2,000 vehicles daily. A national highway system is being developed, and those stretches of multi-lane expressways between major centres already open—2,140 km by the end of 1995—or under construction will eventually form part of four key routes [two running north-south and two east-west]. (1997, 59–60)

The situation is considerably better in the two core regions of China's new economy. The first is the lower Yangzi basin delineated by Shanghai, Nantong, Nanjing, Hangzhou, and Ningbo.[5] The second, to which I now turn for a closer look at one of China's "restless landscapes," is the Pearl River delta.[6]

THE PEARL RIVER DELTA: A RESTLESS LANDSCAPE

The Pearl River Delta (PRD) open economic area is a sub-region of Guangdong Province. In addition to Guangzhou, the provincial capital, it harbors the two special economic zones (SEZ) of Shenzhen and Zhuhai, six so-called leading cities, sixteen county-level cities, and three rural counties, each with its precisely nuanced level of autonomy. In strictly economic terms, however, this development region is structured by the heavily traveled Guangzhou–Hong Kong special administrative region (SAR) corridor and, to a lesser extent, the corridor connecting the provincial capital with Zhuhai SEZ and the Macao SAR.[7] All told, the delta region has a population of around 20 million (out of close to 70 million for the entire province) to which must be added, despite their special administrative status, Hong Kong's 7 million people and another million or so for Macao. This yields a grand total of close to 30 million, a population that currently enjoys the largest per-capita income in the People's Republic. Although Shanghai and the lower Yangzi basin are catching up fast, the PRD continues to be China's economic powerhouse and its most developed region.

The PRD was declared an open economic area in the early 1980s. After lengthy negotiations with the central government, Guangdong Province arranged a deal whereby it could retain all of its surplus earnings after annually transferring the fixed sum of 1 billion yuan to Beijing. At the same time, and again, after considerable debate, the special enclave economy of Shenzhen (along with Zhuhai and a third SEZ, Shantou, located just outside the PRD zone in Guangdong) was established adjacent to Hong Kong. The idea was to attract capital from what was then still the Crown Colony, to learn about the mysteries of free markets, and to encourage the transfer of new technologies from the West.

After a decade of the Cultural Revolution, China's economy had sunk to its lowest point since 1949. People were demoralized, production was sluggish, and the shelves were empty. Ezra Vogel describes the situation well:

> Factory production of consumer good was neglected, because priority was placed on meeting basic industrial needs. Many shelves, even at Nanfang Department Store, the biggest and best in Guangdong, remained empty. When the amount of consumer goods began to increase after the Cultural Revolution, the quality of even the simplest products was still marginal. Light bulbs flickered, clothes had tears, plates had chips, and hot water bottles leaked.
>
> Not only had production stagnated and sometimes stopped; the economy had retrogressed from its position as a system with a moderate amount of regional trade and specialization to one that was more primitive and self-sufficient. This was to make the contrast with the other economies of East Asia, which were in the same period achieving their great takeoffs, all the more dramatic when China was reopened to the outside. (1989, 30–31)

There was a great popular hunger for development, for a better life, for political stability, for an end to ideologically driven campaigns and the daily regimentation of life. These widely shared desires helped launch the reform movement and the extraordinary push for industrialization in the Pearl River delta.[8]

Seizing the day, Hong Kong entrepreneurs shifted most of their light industry into the newly opened and eagerly receptive PRD. They thus took advantage of a seemingly unlimited supply of labor willing to work at wages that were but a fraction of prevailing wages in the Crown Colony, a business climate relatively free of regulations, and local authorities that were exceptionally keen to entice industrialists to their own area by giving them free land, free factories, and free rein.[9] By 1990, 69 percent of gross industrial output in Guangdong was from industries such as garments, toys, and low-end electronics (Lau 1998, table 6.2). For a decade or two, the region was China's Wild West, a case of "primitive accumulation."

In addition to providing industrial capital, Hong Kong also contributed to the emerging system of transportation that would link the SAR to the provincial capital. The province had constructed an impressive bridge across the Pearl River at Humen. It connected to a privately built, six-lane expressway and reduced effective time distance between Hong Kong and Guangzhou to ninety minutes. Besides roads and bridges, there were new container ports, airports, and rail lines, many of them financed via Hong Kong. With these investments in place, the PRD was rapidly growing together as a single

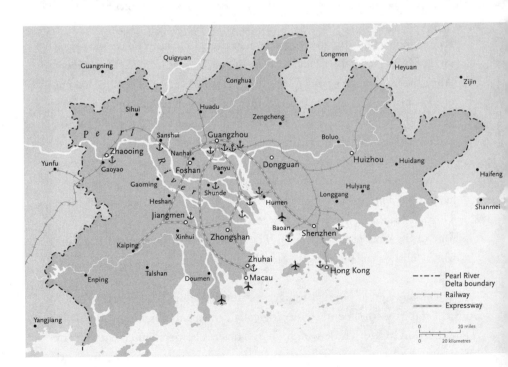

The Pearl River delta urban system

megalopolis, a new species of the genus "city" (Luk 1998; Yeh et al. 2002, chapters 10–12).

The centerpiece of this story is unquestionably Shenzhen (Shiu and Yang 2002, 249). Truly Hong Kong's twin, it was to be a showcase city and an experiment in market-driven urbanization. Despite heavy criticism on the part of earnest socialists whose faith in central planning remained unshaken, "Learning from Shenzhen" soon became the watchword of the day. More than one-third of its 327 km² was to be urbanized, with the remainder initially set aside as nature reserves and for tourism. Its inhabitants having come from all over China in search of work and the good life, Shenzhen was widely regarded as China's most livable city by the end of the millennium, its university one of the best in the country. Twenty percent of China's Ph.D.s were said to be working in Shenzhen (Yeh 2002, 236).

Hong Kong's economy boomed throughout much of the 1980s and 1990s from profits extracted from its cross-border investments. By 1997, however, it was seriously hit by the Asian financial crisis. The collapse of the real estate bubble—Hong Kong prices had reached truly astronomical heights—served as a wake-up call to the new SAR leadership. Other considerations also made strategic planning now a matter of considerable urgency: how to restructure the economy under the watchword of "one country, two systems"; how to reverse the faltering growth rate; how to take advantage of the opening to China; how to address the growing incidence of poverty and unemployment. The familiar formulas of the past were no longer working.

THE "HONG KONG ADVANTAGE"?

The search for a new development strategy is vividly described by Ngai-Ling Sum (2002). Officials turned to the United States for advice, seeking input from experts at Harvard University and the Massachusetts Institute of Technology. The Harvard team counseled an approach that they called "the Hong Kong advantage," based on a continuation of Hong Kong's entrepôt functions of "managing the flows." They envisioned the SAR as increasingly the financial and business service center of the PRD, which was regarded as its natural hinterland. This, of course, was music to the ears of the old Hong Kong merchant elites whose bastion was the chamber of commerce and who had profited handsomely from their cross-border investments. For its part, the MIT team recommended a contrasting approach that envisioned Hong Kong as a leading manufacturing center for the knowledge-based economy of the twenty-first century. This strategic vision also found powerful local adherents. In his own vision for the future, Hong Kong's new chief executive, Tung Chee-hwa, opted to somehow combine the two, though the Hong Kong tycoons in the chamber of commerce, knowing much about trade, finance, and real estate, but little about industrial research and development, would probably have preferred the formula of "the Hong Kong advantage" (Commission on Strategic Development 2000). In the end, Tung Chee-hwa, himself a former business leader, expressed his hope that Hong Kong would grow into a "world class" city rivaling London and New York. Just how this might be done was not clear, however. Although various new institutions were set up to promote MIT's knowledge-based option, on a more immediately practical level, the government sank a billion dollars into a Disneyland theme park that it hoped would attract millions of tourists from the mainland and Taiwan. Due to open in 2005, the park expects 5 million visitors in its first year.

The pressing issue of future relations between Hong Kong and Guangdong Province is far from resolved (Cheung 2002). Although the border between the two remains relatively closed to potential immigrants from the mainland, it has become one of the busiest borders in the world. In 2000, 86 million people and 11 million vehicles crossed over in both directions (Yeh 2002, 328). Anthony Yeh of Hong Kong University believes that despite a clear complementarity of interests, neither local PRD governments nor the government of the SAR are sure about how close they want to be to each other. As intercity competition becomes more intense, should Hong Kong be seen as part of the PRD or the other way around (239)? Because the question remains unresolved, official contacts remain limited and formal. Still, practical issues must be tackled. Visa arrangements, border crossings, and transport efficiency are major concerns. In the first decade of the new millennium, a businessman from the PRD needs four to six weeks to process a visa application to visit the SAR. Environmental conditions such as air and water quality, not to mention livability, are deteriorating on both sides. There is a need to create an efficient intercity rail transit system that would integrate a megalopolis that many still regard as so many different localities strenuously competing against one another. The future may be uncertain, but a pragmatic sense of dealing with problems that require cooperation will probably prevail.

POVERTY AND THE QUESTION OF REGIONAL DISPARITIES

The story of urban-regional development I have tried to sketch in these pages leads from a China that less than thirty years ago was closed to the

world, egalitarian, and poor to one that is open, bound for riches, and increasingly unequal. As I mentioned above, the question of regional disparities is beginning to be of concern to the party-state, and several scholars have
tried to document them (Yang 1997; Wei 2000). The best study of income
inequality and poverty in China was done by Khan and Riskin (2001). It is
based on two sample household surveys (1988 and 1995) conducted by an
international group of economists in collaboration with the Institute of Economics of the Chinese Academy of the Social Sciences. Although the surveys
are inadequate for a detailed analysis of income disparities along regional
lines, they do confirm the impression that there has been a steep increase in
the range of provincial per-capita incomes, especially for rural areas (47).
Khan and Riskin provide insight into rural and urban income differences on
an all-China basis. Overall, they write, "China was among the more unequal
societies in developing Asia by the middle of the 1990s. The Gini ratio [a
measure of inequality] for China in 1995—0.452—is higher than the Gini
ratios for India, Pakistan, and Indonesia, and perhaps about the same as the
Gini ratio for the Philippines" (43).[10] Surprisingly, Gini ratios for individual
provinces were significantly lower than for the country as a whole, with rural
ratios showing greater inequalities than urban incomes (ibid., table 3.9). To
cite only one example: in 1995, rural Guangdong had a Gini ratio of 0.390
and an urban coefficient of 0.316, both of them quite low by international
standards. And other provincial Gini ratios were still lower. The primary explanation for growing rural income inequality, write Khan and Riskin, was the
growth of nonfarm employment (50). But this was concentrated in certain
coastal provinces, and especially near major cities. The all-China measure of
inequality thus reflects this spatial imbalance. By contrast, the most important source of inequality in urban areas was the rental value of privately
owned housing. By 1995 owner-occupied housing had already increased to 11
percent, and the figure is undoubtedly a great deal higher now (145). But if we
turn these data around, it is clear that the vast majority of the urban population lived in rented quarters—hence the growing inequality noted by Khan
and Riskin.

Estimates of the rural population in poverty fell between 1988 and 1995,
with the sharpest declines found in the proportion living in extreme poverty.
In absolute numbers, of course, most of China's poor still live in rural areas, so
that poverty continues to be seen as primarily a rural issue. The incidence of
urban poverty, though rising, is a good deal smaller (ibid., 147). Leaving aside
the so-called "floating population" that by 1995 made up about one-fifth of

official urban residents, most of whom lived at or near poverty levels, urban poverty is strongly correlated with unemployment: in 1995, 8.5 percent of the urban labor force was unemployed, but among the poor, the unemployment ratio was roughly three times as much (148).

The central government is paying increasing attention to these issues, calling for more investments in the central and western regions of the country, and experimenting with concrete measures, such as tax relief and health service provisions, to alleviate the plight of villagers. As Khan and Riskin repeatedly point out, rural poverty is to a large extent a problem of lacking suitable off-the-farm employment. (Paradoxically, the presence of wage employment also increases rural inequality.) Because of the extraordinary rise of township and village enterprises (TVEs) in coastal counties—the primary source of rural wage employment—the next chapter will review the relevant literature on China's urbanization of the countryside.

REGIONALISM AND REGIONAL POLICIES IN PERSPECTIVE

That China's immense territory in the preindustrial era should be understood as a collection of geographical regions articulated by mountains, navigable rivers, and canals is scarcely surprising. Skinner's regions, however, are based primarily on an analysis of urban systems. For this reason, they should properly be called urban trading regions, embedded within a framework of physiographic divisions. Further, over the millennia of its history, China expanded territorially, incorporating many different peoples. There is thus, in addition to physiography and urban markets, a cultural overlay on its regional map, a quilt of regional identities that are distinguished from each other by language, religion, and traditions. From a very early period the country was also linked to the rest of the world via long-distance trade routes both overland and by sea. Land routes would originate or terminate in cities, often the imperial capital, giving special economic importance to these metropolises, and creating a linear pattern of cities along the way. Maritime routes gave special prominence to coastal cities, such as Quanzhou, that acquired a cosmopolitan sheen by virtue of their frequent contact with foreigners. These diverse patterns, finally, had a bureaucratic overlay of provincial and prefectural boundaries.

This traditional and complex regionalism was weakened by modern means of communication and transport that made possible the development of a more integrated space economy. When considering the country's regionalization, we must also take into account the cultural and, above all, political unity of China. Since 1949 the central government has recognized regional diversity by acknowledging certain ethnic minorities, most of whom live in China's border provinces. Altogether these minorities make up about 10 percent of total population, or 130 million. Additionally, the government has allowed for a certain amount of home rule in the so-called autonomous regions and the special administrative regions of Hong Kong and Macao. At the same time it has strengthened the essential unity of the country by mandating a national spoken language, Mandarin, which is taught in the schools, alongside local dialects and regional languages. The ideographic Chinese script is still another unifying force.

Across this variegated regional map of China, Mao Zedong attempted to impose the uniform system of a socialist society, which he envisioned as an egalitarian and spartan utopia. He wanted a strong country that could not only withstand potential foreign invaders but also eventually become a major world power. To do this, China had to industrialize. About this there was little dispute. But military considerations were never far from Mao's mind. For two decades, he had been a military leader, fighting both defensive and offensive battles against the forces of the Guomintang, the Japanese colonial power, and, in Korea, the United States and its allies. The Third Front strategy for industrial location was essentially a defensive strategy. But the relocation of industries into China's interior had still another purpose, both political and symbolic. This was to turn away from the old treaty ports on the coast—cities like Canton (Guangzhou) and Shanghai—with their "cosmopolitan" outlook, and shift the weight of industrial development to China's traditional heartland. This was a nationalist strategy that somewhat resembled Kemal Ataturk's relocation of Turkey's capital from Istanbul to Ankara in the heart of (Asian) Anatolia, or Juscelino Kubitschek's decision to build a new capital city, Brasilia, in the interior of Brazil. All three were geopolitical moves of extraordinary importance in that they rejected a particular self-understanding of the country over which they ruled in favor of a transcendent nationalist image.

The reform policies that followed in the 1980s and 1990s returned the regime's gaze to the coastal provinces and cities. Cosmopolitanism was back in, as economic arguments demoted military and political considerations to second rank. The country needed foreign capital and foreign technologies in order to catch up. The new regional policy, therefore, focused on cities as the strategic locations for this invitation to overseas investors.

The original Ladder-Step Doctrine foresaw the likelihood of growing regional imbalances that would follow upon accelerated economic growth in coastal cities, though admittedly the regional rungs on this ladder did not reflect China's actual regionalization. Still, it is interesting to note that recent five-year plans have signaled a shift in the government's concern, arguing that greater priority should henceforth be given to the country's interior. The prediction of increasing regional inequalities turned out to be true. To what extent this shift in policy will achieve its objective of enticing capital investments into China's interior remains to be seen. In general, initial advantage is hard to override, and regional disparities will no doubt continue for a very long time. Part of this return to China's heartland (if not yet its sparsely inhabited and culturally distinctive periphery) is reflected in the decision to proceed with the Three Gorges Dam project and the recent designation of Chongqing as China's fourth and largest centrally administered city-region.

The pattern of spatially uneven economic growth resulting from the policy of allowing some regions to get rich first had immediate consequences for rural to urban migration, as millions of peasant farmers left their farms in the interior and headed to the coastal cities in search of fortune. This new mobility is the topic of the next chapter.

Construction of the Three Gorges Dam, June 2000

3. Urbanization of the Countryside

Perhaps the most dramatic (and surprising) story of China's transformation during the past twenty-five years has been how significant portions of the country's rural areas have become "urban" in the many meanings of this elusive term. Yu Zhu has referred to this process as *in situ* urbanization (Zhu 1999). The story is usually told as the gradual abandonment of agriculture as a way of life in favor of work in rural industries, but a few scholars have attempted to relate all this to the more encompassing narrative of urbanization in China (Guldin 1997, 2001; Marton 2000).

There is no question that rural industrialization in key coastal regions — most prominently the Pearl River delta, the coastal belt of counties in Fujian Province, the lower Yangzi delta focused on Shanghai, and the development corridor in Liaoning Province connecting Shenyang to the port city of Dalian — has been the most dynamic force in their *economic* transformation. For a complete understanding of the phenomenon, however, we must consider the wider ramifications for spatial, social, and political restructuring.

MULTIPLE FORMS OF URBANIZATION

First, let us take a quick glance at the macro-economic picture of China as a whole at the beginning of the 1990s. Basic reforms in the rural sector began with the de-collectivization of agriculture and the start-up of the so-called household responsibility system in 1983. The abolition of the communes released a flood tide of human inventiveness and energy, and marked the beginning of a frenetic process of rural industrialization. A mere ten years later, it was apparent that a veritable (and peaceful) revolution had occurred that lifted as many as 200 million peasant farmers out of poverty. Lynn T. White sketches its overall dimensions:

By the end of 1990, rural industries accounted for 25 percent of China's total GNP and 60 percent of its rural production. Ninety million people were registered as employed in rural industries, and the real number may have been much higher. Two years later, at the start of 1993, the number of rural employees was reported to be over 105 million. The 1990 figure implies that rural industries employed 87 percent as many people as state industries; and the 1993 figure implies these two sectors were about equal in employment. (1998a, 151)

These extraordinary gains continued throughout the next ten years, though possibly at a less frantic pace. From a spatial and demographic perspective, rural industrialization solved problems for China's planners. It helped slow down the mass migrations to leading cities that took place in developing countries elsewhere, where rural migrants—sometimes refugees from war-torn regions, as in the Sudan—settled in huge, nondescript shantytowns. Outside of China, most rural migrants in poor countries earn their urban livelihood in "informal" work, a sector of relatively unproductive services (Portes, Castells, and Benton 1989). As we shall see in the next chapter, Chinese farmers also migrate to key coastal cities in search of work and a better life, but millions have also headed for the rapidly industrializing rural areas in their vicinity. The result of these changes was the creation—it seems to have occurred almost overnight, but in fact it took more than two decades—of a new urban form in the two major delta regions, the *multi-centric urban field*, and of *peri-urban areas* in the immediate vicinity of medium-sized and large cities that would eventually become integrated with their urban cores. Given the limited descriptive power of a term like *urbanization* that is usually understood only in terms of the demographic growth of predefined "urban" places relative to total population, a more precise, if more complex understanding is called for. Here I propose five dimensions of the multidimensional construct of the urban.

   1. *Administrative urbanization:* In China, as elsewhere, towns and cities are defined administratively, and the criteria that would, for example, turn a village into a town, or a town into a city, are varied and may change over time.[1] A peculiarity in China is that urban residents are identified as such by a *hukou*, or residence permit, that confers on them certain entitlements, such as subsidized food and housing. The central government has tried very hard to limit the number of urban *hukou* but has been only partially successful. About a fifth of the increase in urban (resident) population has come from a reclassification of nonurban places to urban status.

2. *Economic urbanization:* Urbanization brings change in the relative proportions of primary (agricultural, extractive), secondary (manufacturing
industry, construction), and tertiary (trades and services) sectors in the
form of a decline in primary employment and a proportional increase in
secondary and tertiary activities. This structural change toward urban-
type work is usually also reflected in higher productivity per worker across
all sectors. In addition, there may be a growing segment of the population that is receiving a portion of their income from rents, which in
China may derive either from collective ("shareholding") or from private
(household) property (Unger 2002, 169–72). Finally, economic urbanization is often accompanied by an expanding radius of transactions, extend-
ing from local to regional, to national and global.

3. *Physical urbanization:* Village and township acquire an "urban look" as
streets are paved, public spaces are beautified, and housing increasingly
takes the form of multistory apartment buildings (with modern plumb-
ing and indoor bathrooms). There are also factory buildings, new shop-
ping complexes, recreation facilities, hotels, medical clinics, new and
improved schools. Finally, excessive damage to the environment, from
belching smokestacks to dwindling ground water supplies and rivers
that have turned into malodorous sewers, has become prominent in many
parts of China.

4. *Sociocultural urbanization:* Everyday life is transformed. Large numbers of
newcomers work in local factories, construction, and whatever remains
of increasingly specialized farming operations. Because they are outsiders to local communities with different customs and languages, their
presence may give rise to new forms of social tension. Furthermore, the
relatively simple social stratification of peasant life (especially as it existed under revolutionary communism) is giving place to new, more complex forms.[2] Finally, there are new forms of individual and household
consumption and uses of leisure (see chapter 5). The technologies of
computer and cell phone—the information revolution—are among the
visible instruments shaping the unbounded city.

5. *Political urbanization:* Even in a party-state such as China, political change
is associated with urbanization. The government has been forced to
decentralize decision-making power to local authorities. Even though
they are not elected, they must act in the name of local populations and
in their interests. New structures of power emerge, with strong linkages
between local officials and business elites. Jean Oi (1999) refers to this

model of governance as local corporatism. But with the power of new business elites in the ascendant, the power monopoly of the local party-state is waning. Power must now be shared.

AN ENDOGENOUS DEVELOPMENT

Many accounts of China's transformation, not least official Chinese accounts, stress the role of foreign capital in the transformation of an agrarian into an urban society. Much of this capital has come from Hong Kong (since 1997 officially a part of the PRC) and Taiwan, which Chinese sources systematically refer to as a "province." There have also been other sources of investment in coastal regions, coming from Southeast Asia, Japan, Korea, the United States, and the European Union. Even so, rural industrialization, which has been the driving force behind the complex urbanization processes sketched above, can only be described as a form of *endogenous* development. Although outside capital has played a predominant role in the Pearl River delta as well as in parts of Fujian Province, investment impulses even in these regions were guided by local officials, and as we shall see, there have also been impressive instances of flamboyant local entrepreneurship. And elsewhere in rural China, overall development (including urbanization) is chiefly a result of local initiatives.

With the conversion of the countryside into multi-centric urban fields, China's experience can be broadly ascribed to six causal factors:

1. Rural population densities that are equal to and even exceed metropolitan densities in Western countries
2. A huge excess supply of labor that can be more productively employed in nonagricultural work
3. Historical antecedents, such as ancient craft traditions, that favor industrialization
4. Resourceful local leadership in both entrepreneurial (risk-taking) and broader developmental roles
5. Widespread entrepreneurial talent and promotional savvy on the part of local households that perceive new opportunities for moving out of poverty and underemployment on a constantly shrinking land base
6. High rates of both collective and household savings, and their reinvestment in both productive facilities and social infrastructure, including housing

It is true that rural urbanization has been occurring chiefly in the vicinity of large cities, in regions with good and constantly improving transport connections and commercial linkages. This is certainly the case of southern Jiangsu Province, which is described below. But urban proximity is not, in my view, a primary explanation of why, out of all the "developing" countries in the world, China is the only one (with the possible exception of communist Vietnam [see DiGregorio 2001]) where rural industrialization has shaped new urban configurations, the only country where rural industrialization has been truly transformative. The six factors identified above may not, in the end, tell us why China's experience has been exceptional—why, for instance, something similar has not occurred in Java, Malaysia, or the Philippines. But they will certainly shed light on the most dramatic and largely unanticipated result of China's reform period.

I would like to home in on one of the major regions of this transformation with a few bits of data for rural Jiangsu Province, covering two time periods separated by twenty years (Marton 2000, tables 3.2 and 3.3). Straddling the Yangzi River, Jiangsu is a large province adjoining Shanghai that contributes about 18 percent to China's industrial product. The following dramatic statistics are for the province as a whole, even though much of rural Jiangsu's transformation has been concentrated in the southern portion of the province, popularly known as Sunan.

In constant prices adjusted for inflation, the total value of Jiangsu's industrial output rose from 6 billion yuan in 1978 to 960 billion in 1998, or from 29 percent to 86 percent of total output. In 1978, there were 56,000 industrial enterprises; that number skyrocketed to 105,000 by 1988. A decade later, with failures and amalgamations, rural enterprises in Jiangsu settled down at about 64,000, with a thirteenfold increase in productivity. Also noteworthy is the absolute increase in agricultural production, from 13 billion yuan in 1978 to 50 billion two decades later. An impressive absolute gain, however, represented a *relative* decline from 62 percent in 1978 to only 4 percent by the end of the period. Finally, the output of a category of "other" production, including construction, transportation, and commerce, not only overtook agriculture by 1998 but actually rose to more than double the output in primary (agricultural) production.

A similar story is told with Jiangsu's employment statistics: *down* in agriculture from 19 million to 15 million (signifying enormous increases in productivity per worker and suggesting a major shift out of basic grains into high-value-added production for urban markets), and *up* in industry from 2 million to nearly 5 million, and in the "other" (service) category from 1 million to nearly 7 million, for a combined "urban" employment shift from 3 million to 12 million.[3]

Changes such as these are duplicated in other key regions of China. To see how they occurred, I turn now to the six causal factors listed above, illustrating with specific examples the kinds of explanation that are encountered in the literature.

High Rural Population Densities and "Surplus" Labor

China's rural population densities, especially in coastal regions, are comparable to metropolitan-wide densities in other countries.[4] For the lower Yangzi delta, Andrew Marton (2000, 70) reports rural densities ranging from 750 to 1,260 persons per square kilometer, and according to Yu Zhu (1999, 159), the twenty-seven coastal counties of Fujian Province have an average density of 595 people per square kilometer. Because of large-scale in-migration to these areas following the relaxation of the *hukou* system, these already very high densities have actually increased still further. Densities of this magnitude presented both a problem and an opportunity. The problem was that agriculture alone, especially if concentrated on the cultivation of basic grains, provided only a meager subsistence to farming households. Studying Jinjiang county in Fujian Province, Zhu (1999, 118–19) points out that per-capita arable land, which was still 1.23 *mu* (0.08 ha) in 1949, had dropped dangerously to 0.56 *mu* (0.04 ha) by 1978, leaving large numbers of farmers on the edge of starvation. He observes that

> the problem of rural surplus labor and the necessity of developing rural non-agricultural activities had long been realized by China's central government. As early as 1952 the Central Employment Committee of China pointed out that there were a large number of surplus laborers in the rural area, and proposed a range of measures to solve this problem. One of the measures was to promote sideline activities and handicraft industry. In 1958, during the People's Commune campaign, the Central Committee of the CCP put forward "the industrialization of communes," suggesting that industry should be greatly promoted. (119)

But sideline and industrial production were subordinated to the overriding objective of self-reliance in agriculture, especially in grains, as symbolized by the official slogan: "take grain as the key link and seek all-round development" (120). Nevertheless, some enterprises producing machinery, hardware, and construction materials were established in Jinjiang during the 1960s, and by 1978 the county had a total of 1,141 commune and brigade enterprises employing 52,000 rural laborers who made up 15 percent of the rural work force. "In short," writes Zhu, "the foundations of the TVEs (township and village industries, the "collective" sector) had already been laid down before 1978, but they played only limited roles in the rural economy" (121).

If high rural densities and rural underemployment were the problem, the challenge was to switch from low-intensity farming to more productive industries without abandoning local villages, and so to begin the transformative process (and promise) of *in situ* urbanization.[5]

Historical Antecedents

The Jinjiang story, which could be repeated in numerous other counties, clearly shows that the explosive growth of rural industries after 1983 was not the result of an inexplicable flowering of local entrepreneurship and

Rural industrialization in Jinjiang County, Fujian Province, 1994. This area has since been consolidated and made less polluting.

technical knowhow but had its origins in collective production at brigade (village) and commune (township) levels during the previous two decades. Although the commune system was disestablished in 1983, and farming was returned to the so-called responsibility system based on household production, the legislative basis of collective property persisted and provided the basis for the remarkable upsurge in rural productivity that was to follow (White 1998a, 113).

If the Maoist experiment in collectivism had put down a foundation for rural industrialization, then rural craft-based production, a centuries-old tradition in many parts of coastal China, provides an even deeper explanation.[6] During imperial times, for example, Xiqiao, a township in the Pearl River delta, had evolved a cottage industry of silk spinning and the weaving of silk into cloth. Mechanized in the latter part of the nineteenth century, local textile production continued throughout the republican period. Under revolutionary communism, these home-based industries were collectivized and their scale was enlarged. Then, in 1984,

> several risk-taking technicians and workers from the three collective textile factories quit their jobs and struck out on their own, starting up tiny private factories containing a few electric looms apiece. With cloth in very short supply in China in the mid-1980s, whatever the tiny new factories produced was snapped up by customers. Seeing the profits that could be made, neighbors rushed to open their own enterprises. In some of the township's villages, by the late 1980s close to half of all the families owned factories. (Unger 2002, 133)

Because rising labor costs and pollution curtailed the cultivation of mulberry bushes and the rearing of silkworm cocoons, textile production in Xiqiao soon switched to artificial fibers. And because it was the first locale in southern China to produce large quantities of synthetic-fiber cloth for the open market, the township "rapidly attracted purchasing agents from garment factories throughout the country. By the 1990s they were arriving each year by the thousands, and they became the eyes and ears of Xiqiao's factory owners, enabling local producers to keep abreast of market trends across China" (134). It may be worthwhile to recall that Western Europe's industrial revolution drew on similar century-old traditions and collective memories.[7] In a passage that foreshadows what we now know about the flourishing delta regions of China and their traditional skills in silks and ceramics, Fernand Braudel describes the weavers and traders of medieval Flanders:

By the mid-eleventh century, the weavers of the flatlands had come to live in the urban centres. The population increased, large agricultural estates prospered, and the textile industry kept workshops busy from the banks of the Seine and Marne to the Zuyder Zee.

It was all to culminate in the dazzling fortune of Bruges. By 1200, this city, together with Ypres, Thourout and Messines, was included in the circuit of Flemish fairs. This in itself made Bruges a more important place: she was receiving foreign merchants, her industry was thriving and her trade was reaching England and Scotland where she found the wool needed for her looms and for re-export to the cloth-making towns of Flanders. (Braudel 1992, 99)

The period of which Braudel writes was contemporaneous with the two Song dynasties in China when especially the lower Yangzi valley had a flourishing, rapidly urbanizing economy, with dozens of new towns and cities springing up amid its fertile, rice-producing terraces. Regional centers began to specialize in products for which they were renowned. Suzhou, for instance, was famous for its brocade, embroidery, and iron cookware. Some counties specialized in tea production. And as markets, even for daily necessities, expanded, and local specialization continued, communities became more interdependent (Heng 1999, 183–86). This ancient tradition is feeding contemporary rural industrialization in coastal China.

Resourceful Local Leadership

Ownership patterns in rural China today are a mixture of collective, joint-venture partnerships, and private. Although the mix appears to be changing in favor of private ownership (individual or household), collective property is still the dominant sector in most regions. Moreover, village administrations, though increasingly in the hands of popularly elected officials, do not act solely on matters affecting the general welfare, such as local road construction and the provision of public services. They also allocate public lands to dedicated uses for generating income (e.g., they can lease land to private developers for the construction of a golf course) as well as make direct investments in economic ventures. The quality of local leadership—its resourcefulness, its entrepreneurial drive—is thus a decisive force in the current transition. This was the case especially at the beginning of the reform process, when the option of private enterprise in a socialist economy was still regarded as something beyond the pale.

Here I will relate two stories about the quality of local leadership. The first comes from a village (now town) in Dalian municipality, a major port in northeastern China (Hoffman and Liu 1997). Beile village based its growth and economic diversification on the Shenyang-Dalian expressway, built in 1991, that passed alongside it. According to a local source, Beile's present prosperity is to a large extent due to one man's ability to provide the right kind of leadership at the right time. That man is Chi Fusheng, Beile's former party secretary and, at the time of his interview, the village head. In 1984, led by Chi Fusheng, Beile village invested in a textile factory.[8] Under his skillful management, the factory proved so successful that it soon sprouted other enterprises, all of them either under the collective ownership of the village or, in some cases, joint-venture projects. These were variously engaged in manufacturing sewing machine needles, textiles, furniture, or chemicals, dyeing, and food processing. Eight years after this successful launch, Beile organized itself as an economic conglomerate (*jituan*) and set up the general company headed by Chi Fusheng, who also continued as village head.

> Most significant, however, was the construction of the expressway that runs right next to the village. Manager Chi actively encouraged these new conditions, sent investigators out to the surrounding area to determine community needs, decided they would build a large commodities market, and then applied for a permit from the Dalian Municipal Government. In 1995, after the market was opened and the Dalian Government recognized the area's economic development and its ability to attract and support surplus labor from surrounding areas, Beile village became a small town. Previously Beile Village was part of Ershi Lipu *zhen*, but now it is called Beile *zhen* [township]. (161)

With its new administrative status, and an infusion of cash from the province, Beile bought other villages' land and incorporated the surrounding area in its administrative reach. This expanded its population to around ten thousand residents, but Chi Fusheng, who in the meantime had been promoted to head the new township, expressed the hope that its population would eventually reach three times this number, the official size of a small city. Clearly, as Hoffman and Liu conclude, the "interplay of policy reform and entrepreneurial skills of local leaders is affecting the type of rural urbanization and economic diversification a village experiences" (ibid.).

My second story centers on Xiqiao, the Pearl River delta township of twenty-six villages referred to earlier. One of these villages, Lianxin, has a resident population of 3,550 plus 6,000 migrant workers, most of whom are working in its 300 small textile plants (Unger 2002, 150–52). Most of them are household enterprises (there are 920 resident households in Lianxin). I have already mentioned how they began with the first breakaway group from the collective. The village administration did not try to hinder private enterprise during the mid-1980s, when it was not yet clear whether Beijing would sanction such initiatives. At the same time, however, it sought actively to develop publicly owned industry. In neighboring Nanzhuan, a township that had specialized in floor and wall tiles, and was dominating the south China market, the Lianxin leaders found an example they hoped to emulate. In 1991

> the [new] Lianxin village Party secretary had the village government borrow close to a hundred million yuan in bank loans to erect a vast tile factory. He imported advanced machinery from West Germany and hired specialists in ceramic tile manufacture from other parts of China. The facility is of truly awesome size, with huge halls containing computerized conveyor-belt kilns the length of football fields. In the early 1990s a property boom was in full swing in Guangdong, and this was generating a voracious demand for construction tiles. . . . By 1997 the township contained twenty-three behemoth tile factories. (151–52)

Success was rewarded, writes Unger. The village party secretary was elevated to serve simultaneously as the party secretary and new political kingpin of Xiqiao Township. In departing Lianxin, he was able to select his own successors, choosing for the post of village head and village party secretary two local businessmen who had done well in textile manufacturing (152). In Lianxin, the party, local government, and business were beginning to converge.

The critical role of local government and thus of its leadership in guiding and even directly intervening in the development process cannot be overemphasized. According to Jean Oi (1999), "higher levels of government . . . have encouraged collectively owned township and village enterprises to adopt new forms of management to make them more competitive and efficient" (81). Just as Manager Chi began acting like the village CEO when Beile incorporated itself as a general company, so other forms of local state corporatism are emerging throughout China (97). Among them are leasing (*zulin*), shareholding (*gufenzhi*), and conglomerates (*jituan*) (81). All of them are potential sources of revenues, which can be either reinvested to expand or upgrade production or spent on projects that are deemed to be of public benefit. "It is common for highly industrialized villages to build schools, housing, movie theatres, and community centers for their members," writes Oi. "In the mid-1980s, some provided the community with free water, electricity, and liquid fuel as well as subsidies for education ranging from 600 to 3,000 yuan for each student who passed the college entrance examination. . . . In one of China's most industrialized villages, over 2 million yuan was spent per year in the late 1980s on various subsidies, excluding services; this village was earning over 30 million yuan in profits" (80).

Entrepreneurial Talent and Promotional Savvy

Private enterprise was beginning to take off in the second half of the 1990s, and before long, businesspeople were invited to join the Communist Party. Early innovators in starting businesses outside the framework of the state were places like Xiqiao Township (already discussed) and the coastal city of Wenzhou in Zhejiang Province. In Maoist times, Wenzhou had had a somewhat dubious reputation, being suspected of capitalist propensities. Today, it is hailed as a model.

> Most striking was the "Wenzhou model." . . . Wenzhou, despite its urban population of over half a million, was safely sequestered for economic experiments. No railway reached there, and during early reforms there was no regular air service. Partly because of extensive illicit contacts between Wenzhou boats and those from Taiwan, and especially because of the city's isolation, this was an apt place for daring tests of PRC capitalism. The late 1980s saw a spate of books by reformist intellectuals about Wenzhou. About 80 percent of Wenzhou capital was by the late 1980s private, rather than state or collective. Private Wenzhou banks loaned credit quite easily. Over 100,000 salespeople, scattered throughout China, launched strenuous marketing efforts on behalf of Wenzhou traders. . . . Models proliferated. Closer to Shanghai, the "Sunan model" of South Jiangsu was mainly distinguished by collective enterprises. Aside from the Sunan, Wenzhou, and Gengche models in East China, the south had its "Zhujiang (Pearl River) model" around Guangzhou. Intellectuals in the north mooted a "Langfang model." . . . These were all named after the counties or prefectures in which various experiments took place. . . . The rural actors were not making models, however; they were making money. (White 1998a, 146)[9]

The following anecdote, also drawn from White, illustrates a phenomenon repeated thousands of times up and down the China coast.

A town in Tongxian county, Zhejiang, became "the kingdom of ducks" after one of its peasants found that the local environment was superb for breeding fowl. He earned 30,000 yuan a year by the late 1980s ("nearly ten times the income of the Zhejiang provincial governor," a PRC paper noted). Following suit, his fellow villagers all soon raised ducks. A majority of families in that village during 1989 earned 10,000 yuan a year. The boom also led to industrial diversification, because the village leaders founded a factory producing duck feed. As a local tycoon put it, "Believe me, we've really become masters of production. . . . That government officials have become our servants is a great change, brought about by reform." (109)

It took one farmer to break through the mold of past constraints and in doing so, to assume both political and economic risks. But as soon as his neighbors smelled success, they rushed to imitate what he had done, and village officials in both Xiqiao and Tongxian bent, as they say, with the wind. There are leaders and followers in both, but once the dam is broken, the desire for riches on the part of an impoverished peasantry cannot be held back. Specialization is a natural outgrowth of this pattern, because followers, being more cautious, are often unwilling to venture onto unbeaten paths. They produce what their village or township is already good at producing: ducks, textiles, shoes, tiles, machine parts. In a highly competitive environment, some entrepreneurs become more successful than others and at some point may be willing to try to break into international markets. But that is another story. Whatever the case, innovator or follower, China is not short of entrepreneurial talent.

Jonathan Unger has asked whether there is a specifically Chinese pattern of entrepreneurship, such as he found in Xiqiao (2002, 138–41). Citing studies from Jinjiang township in Fujian province and a 1993 survey in Taiwan, he concludes that there is indeed such a pattern. He describes it as a risk-taking initiative when opportunities opened for small-scale manufacturing; a turn to partnerships to gain an initial foothold as a small manufacturer; a tendency to dissolve these partnerships eventually in favor of family-based firms; a role for the spouse in supervising some of the firm's internal operations; and a propensity for the proprietor to save and reinvest out of profits in order to upgrade and expand the business rather than rely on bank loans. "It is a pattern that has strong social roots in China," he writes. "But we can also expect that as in Xiqiao, the entrepreneurs who are able to transcend the family-firm tradition will, overall, do better" (140).

High Rates of Household Savings, and Collective
and Private Reinvestment in Infrastructure

Kunshan is a county-level city in Sunan (southern Jiangsu Province) approximately midway between Shanghai and Suzhou. Within the Kunshan administrative area, there are 20 towns and 463 villages scattered over 467 km² of arable land. Its resident population is close to 600,000. Between 1979 and 1996 the average *annual* rate of increase of its industrial output was 33 percent. Much of this increase was self-financed (Marton 2000, 7–8).

Household savings deposits in Kunshan were extraordinary, rising from a mere 38 million yuan in 1980 to 5.8 billion yuan in 1998, which on a percapita basis is equal to about 10,000 yuan. At the same time, fixed assets in the county, largely funded by local borrowing, rose from 18 million to 5.8 billion yuan (162). Nearly 80 percent of this industrial investment flowed into town- and village-level collective and private enterprises. According to Andrew Marton (2000),

> Local control of such investments by rural cadres was exercised through community government management of the profits and other funds of town and village enterprises and the manipulation of loan portfolios of local banks. Another key element of capital flows in Kunshan was the disbursement of net earnings of rural enterprises. . . . Local enterprises reinvested 40.4 per cent of their net earnings in enterprise improvement and expansion. A further 19.8 per cent of net earnings were remitted directly to local governments, most of which was available for other investments in local development. A portion of the average 27.1 per cent paid in taxes was also available to town level governments for budgetary expenditures. Officials in Kunshan, bent on promoting pet projects, also leaned on local financial institutions to obtain loans. While lending was supposed to be based on commercial considerations, much of it was in fact politically motivated. (163)

Methods of raising capital for local investment were often ingenious. In Jinjiang county, Fujian, for example, an enterprising farmer named Lin Toqiu wanted to open up a shoe factory in his house. This was at the onset of the reforms in 1979. He did so by raising 100,000 yuan from fourteen farmers he knew. Those farmers, by virtue of their investment, also became the first group of workers in his factory, a joint shareholding enterprise. After more than ten years in production, farmer Lin's factory was worth 2.4 million yuan in fixed capital and another million in working capital. By 1991 he was producing between three thousand and five thousand pairs of shoes every day (Zhu 1999, 126–27).

Elsewhere, economic cooperatives have been set up, as for instance in Nanhai county, Guangdong, to manage township lands under a shareholding system. The township is a former commune, and even though it has been de-collectivized in principle, the practice of collective land holdings lingers on. Township residents are given certificate shares for the land they contribute to the cooperative, but the allocation of shares is not, as one might think, based on the number of *mu* or hectares each household contributes but on another basis altogether. In Jiancun, for example,

> each infant whose parents are native to the village receives one share at birth. The native young people hold one share up to the age of 17; those between the ages of 18 and 35 hold two shares; when they reach the ages of 36 they are given an extra share and hold three shares until the age of 55; and every native member of the community over 55 holds four shares. A person's shares disappear when he or she dies, and a female loses her shares when she marries out of the community, though she gains an equivalent amount of shares in her husband's village when she enters it. A village family that moves away similarly loses its shares and dividends—village residence is necessary to remain part of the community—but the shares reappear if the family moves back and thereby re-enters community life. (Unger 2002, 160–61)

Dividends derive from renting out the land for agri-business, fish ponds, agricultural fields, golf courses, or any other use. In Xiqiao, cash distributions in 1996 ranged from 1,000 to 10,000 yuan, and in some townships distributions were considerably higher. This is an annual rental income, and for an extended family household of five or six, the total may in some cases run up to 100,000 yuan. Some of this may be reinvested in housing and education, some may be spent on consumer products such as a refrigerator or washing machine, and some may be ventured in local real estate or in a factory. It is clear that under conditions of *in situ* urbanization, with the very high population densities that are involved, and under conditions of rapid economic expansion, people who only three decades ago were subsistence peasants can now enjoy a comfortable urban style of life.

As Dorothy Solinger points out, however, rural industries' ability to absorb labor began to decline in the latter half of the 1990s. Employment in this sector dropped by 17 million in 1998 alone, and by almost 33 million throughout the 1990s. Following China's accession to the World Trade Organization in 2001, rural industries may be unable to compete successfully with larger scale, better managed foreign firms in the domestic market, and the end of *in situ* urbanization—so successful in the 1980s and 1990s—may well be in sight (Solinger 2003, 85). Another observer, Michael Leaf, confirms this view. According to Leaf, township and village enterprises (TVEs) have been going through a shakeout in recent years, with the most successful firms expanding and privatizing, while the less successful are standing idle (personal communication). These are alarming observations. We may recall, however, that rural industrialization during the past two decades was essentially a transitional phenomenon that helped coastal regions in China transform themselves into a pattern of dispersed urbanization. Despite increasing competition, TVEs still play a vital role in the local economy and, indeed, in the country as a whole. How they will fare in the future remains to be seen.

In the foregoing pages, I have focused on some of the conditions favoring rural industrialization and on its strong roots in Chinese history, leadership administrative ability, entrepreneurship, technical knowhow, and high rates of household and collective saving. That is to say, I have described it as a form of endogenous development. It is nevertheless obvious that this is not a purely economic story but the story of a countryside changing itself through its own efforts into a new kind of urban phenomenon and a new way of life.

> We have seen an instance of administrative urbanization in the case of Beile village (*cun*), which became a township (*zhen*).
>
> In Jiangsu province, we have seen a highly productive agricultural sector decline in relative terms as urban production and employment became dominant in the local economy.
>
> I have made numerous references to the physical conversion of villages and townships that within a relatively short time acquired an urban look, sporting high-rise apartments, fancy villas, paved streets, new schools, restaurants, and cinemas, as their inhabitants increasingly adopted an urban style of life.
>
> I have drawn attention to a change in social stratification and the increasing presence of "strangers"—migrant workers—in the midst of established communities of what were once peasant farmers who are now drawing a growing proportion of their income from rental properties.
>
> Finally, I have alluded to local elections and hence to the beginnings of

popular self-government and new structures of power favoring local business interests.

In some parts of China, then, a new urban form is emerging, which I have called a *multi-centric urban field*. Despite its increasingly urban character, the multi-centric urban field still retains some of its rural qualities. Here and there, intensive farming is carried on in the shadow of factories and apartment buildings, and old patterns of collective property persist in the form of "economic shareholding cooperatives." In the remainder of this chapter, I will take a closer look at two aspects of this metamorphosis: the emerging form of local governance and the special case of peri-urban areas—that is, rural districts on the edges of larger cities that are gradually becoming absorbed into the urban grid.

THE CASE OF LOCAL ELECTIONS

Gregory Guldin (2001) gives a vivid account of an election in a rural county south of Kunming, Yunnan. The business at hand was the election of the members of a village committee. Its legal basis was a law passed in 1987 by the National People's Congress, authorizing such elections.

> When we visited Eshan [county] in October 1999 [writes Guldin], the village government complexes were festooned with banners encouraging the election process, and local officials described a framework of universal suffrage to all over 18 years, a villager-led nomination process, and a secret ballot. And as befits these "elections with Chinese characteristics" in a society built around extended families, proxy voting powers were given to household heads to represent others in the family when casting ballots. Local businessmen have also been nominated to become village heads and other village committee officials, often because "people think businessmen are cleverer than most folks." (93)

Such elections have become routine in the 930,000 villages of rural China. For the first time in the country's history, elections allow villagers to choose their own leadership.[10] True, the village secretary of the party is still an appointed position. But, at least at the local level, the party is no longer in complete control. Increasingly, the secretary will have to negotiate with elected members of the village government or enter into collusion with them in an "amphibious" version of the party-state.[11] There are even tenuous signs that the electoral process may eventually be extended to some of the country's

47,100 townships where elections are presently forbidden (278).[12] In an essay on village democracy in Guangdong Province—a province lagging by a decade behind other parts of China where the self-government movement was initiated much earlier—Richard Levy (2003) concludes that "the Chinese Party and state have obviously invested considerable prestige and resources in developing this movement with its attendant elections and in trying to balance control and legitimacy. The elections, by legitimizing the notion of self-government and the act of voting, themselves transformed the political discourse in China. Imperfect though they are, village elections continue to be implemented incrementally and become increasingly well established" (52).

THE CASE OF PERI-URBAN AREAS

Observers are taking an increased interest in rural districts surrounding large cities that are themselves expanding (Webster and Muller 2002; Leaf 2002; Zhang, Zhao, and Tian 2003). They are suburbs consisting of villages, which are on the road to becoming physically and administratively indistinguishable from the central city. The story of their urbanization has been told throughout this chapter; what is perhaps new is the process by which such villages are incorporated into the city.

Quanzhou is an ancient maritime port in Fujian Province. Its traditional urban core is small—only about 250,000 people living on 17 km²—but its administrative area extends over several counties that harbor a resident population, not counting migrants, of 6.6 million. Since 1980 several administrative villages on its perimeter have abandoned agriculture and have become urbanized in all but name. More recently, some of them have been incorporated as full-blown urban neighborhoods within Quanzhou City. One of these villages is Chengzhong. Its party secretary briefly describes the process:

> The village committee changed to a neighbourhood committee in 2000. The villagers all received urban *hukou* then as well. There are about 100 old houses still in the district, but most have been torn down and replaced with higher density housing. It used to be one neighbourhood but now it has been split into four. There are about 1,500 original villagers still living here, and about 500 other people have bought houses here. Most of the villagers now have businesses. Since this is effectively now the city centre, there is no more agricultural activity. In fact, this village urbanised early, beginning in 1979 and continuing through the 1980s. By 1993 it was completely urbanised, and the reconstruction took place in 1998. (Anderson 2003, 32)

Typically, as Samantha Anderson explains, a village will begin to industrialize and, in the course of this process, sell off its land to build factories as well as for other uses, such as warehousing, usually in a special industrial zone. With the new prosperity, old courtyard houses are gradually replaced with self-built, three-story houses. Eventually, the municipal government may decide that the time has come for the village to be merged with the urban core. A development company is established, and the old village housing is torn down and replaced with apartment blocks, while infrastructure is upgraded. Finally, the village committee is given its new urban designation as "resident neighborhood committee," and villagers (but not the migrant workers who may live there) receive an urban *hukou*.[13] This final stage in the process, however, must be approved by the provincial government (ibid.). For some places, this process turns out to be quite lucrative. Dongtu village, for example, became an urban neighborhood in 2001. The local neighborhood committee now runs two development companies and has 5–6 million yuan invested in real estate developments.

Central street of Dong Mei village, Quanzhou, Fujian Province, 2003

"Villages like Chengzhou and Dongtu are indistinguishable physically from the urban core," writes Anderson, "although Dongtu, like villages further from the historical core, has a large migrant population. . . . Villagers rent out rooms and apartments to migrants who work in the city in construction or service industry, or run their own businesses. This distinguishes them from migrants living in villages more on the edge of the city, who are predominantly factory workers" (ibid.).

One such "more distant" village is Huoju, which lies south of the Jin River, about a fifteen-minute bus ride from Quanzhou's city center. Huoju has not as yet been administratively absorbed into the city. In 2001 it had a population of 1,629 residents and an additional 5,000 registered migrants who for the most part lived in the dormitories of the Huoju Industrial Estate. However, the estate employs 20,000 workers, most of whom are also migrants. In this village, migrants both registered and unregistered outnumber traditional residents nine to one. Perhaps this is the reason why Huoju has not yet been privileged to be incorporated as an urban neighborhood. Migrants are considered "temporary" population.

Huoju earns about 2 million yuan in rents from its former farm lands that have been leased to the factories. By Chinese standards, it is a prosperous place. Incorporated in the industrial estate is a street lined with restaurants, clothing stores, medical clinics, household goods stores, cell phone outlets, photography studios, a wedding dress shop, a couple of jewelry shops, and a video and book rental shop. As someone observed in a similar village on the outskirts of Xiamen, "We live like city people now; we can get everything. Our village is almost a city" (Shi 1997, 149).[14]

A CASE OF CHINESE EXCEPTIONALISM?

Like so many stories in China, the story of rural transformation is an unfinished one. Its effects on the environment have, on the whole, been terrible. In human terms, it has been marked by corruption that has wormed its way into the lowest levels of the Chinese bureaucracy. Its promise of greater democracy has been stalled, as the extension of village elections to the next higher township level is fiercely resisted by the party *nomenklatura* ensconced there. It has encouraged a savage localism, in which material values take precedence over any other consideration. One can only hope that this period of "primitive accumulation" will soon be succeeded by a more balanced process of change in which a new measure of civic order will be reintroduced.

The real question is why *in situ* urbanization happened as rapidly as it did, and why it happened only in China and practically nowhere else in the developing world. In other countries, international aid agencies and local nongovernmental organizations struggle to introduce some principles and practices of community development to villages that have been bypassed by development, generally to no avail. Lacking an economic base, these socially motivated programs have little purchase. No one in China is talking about community development. Things are happening in ways that the community development literature, which is extensive, does not address.[15] There is an energetic local leadership. There is entrepreneurship. There are organizational linkages that permit party and locality to join in a common enterprise. There are inventive ways that lead to the incorporation of a whole village as a commercial firm. Outside investors are made welcome, but the local savings rate is one of the highest in the world.

These very real achievements, which should be the envy of villages around the globe, had their antecedents in the Maoist period. They are a result of a long period of experimentation with collectivism, rural sideline production, the fostering of local leadership. Today's "restless landscapes" are the positive outfall of many of Mao's great policy failures, from the communalization of village China to the Great Leap Forward. Rural industries got their start under Mao but were held back by the mistaken belief that China's number-one priority was self-sufficiency in grain. Once the lid was off, however, and collective and private enterprises were allowed to flourish, they did.

Left out from all of this discussion, but inherently a part of this story of becoming urban, is the mass migratory movement from countryside to city, or to the rapidly urbanizing townscapes and villagescapes that are part of this epic-in-the-making. This is the subject of the next chapter.

4. New Spatial Mobilities

Given the mostly hostile attitudes among urban residents toward migrants, and the government's reluctance to let people freely choose where they would like to live and work, it is perhaps useful to remind ourselves that Chinese peasants are not naturally "rooted" in their villages, any more than agriculturalists elsewhere in the world. Nor have they only recently discovered that moving to cities is a way of improving their prospects in life. Historically, the Chinese are an enterprising, highly mobile people. Beginning in the mid-nineteenth century large numbers of Chinese, especially from Guangdong and Fujian Provinces, emigrated to Southeast Asia, Australia, Canada, and the United States. They and their offspring number in the tens of millions. Many migrants also streamed into China's cities, such as the newly industrializing Shanghai and the trading emporium of Hankou.

By 1800 Hankou was already a thriving river port at the confluence of the Yangzi and Han Rivers, 1,000 km upstream from Shanghai. Its population stood at approximately 1 million. For another fifty years numbers continued to swell, reaching an estimated 1.5 million—a figure that made Hankou the largest city in the world at the time. But the devastation caused by the Taiping Rebellion led to a dramatic drop in population, from which the city had barely recovered by the end of the century. William Rowe (1989) refers to Hankou as a city of sojourners and immigrants. His study of migrants shows many similarities to urban migrations in China today. He divides Hankou migrants into three groups (214–23):

> Those who came to stay, driven from the countryside by disasters such as political violence, bandits, floods, and famine. For the most part, this group was composed of illiterate peasants.
> Those drawn chiefly from Hankou's hinterland, who intended to remain

in the city more or less permanently. Rowe calls them sojourners. In contrast to the first group, many of them had working farms to which they would return periodically. In the city, they worked mainly as unskilled laborers, artisans, and petty traders.

Temporary migrants who came to Hankou in search of personal advancement and riches. Many of this upwardly mobile group were traders and long-distance merchants. Some were literati hoping for an administrative appointment. On the lower end of the social scale, there were the thousands of boatmen who congregated in the city's busy port.

Rowe argues that, like many large cities in Europe, Hankou failed to reproduce itself, needing immigrants for its survival and prosperity. In this city of migrants, males outnumbered females two to one. The birth rate was consequently low, while mortality rates were high, as epidemics periodically ravaged the city, especially after the annual spring floods.

Despite coming from many different parts of China, and speaking different dialects, migrants in this polyglot city lived in relative peace with one another. Local origin served as an ordering principle. Typically, migrants lived in ethnic enclaves that provided for mutual support and protection. And many jobs—artisans, boatmen, laborers, peddlers—were ethnically typed as well. Nevertheless, a distinction was frequently made between "locals" and "outsiders"; the latter were regarded with deep suspicion.

Overall, the image of nineteenth-century Hankou is one of fluidity, of the peaceful incorporation of newcomers with strong continuing ties to their native places. Roughly speaking, the city was divided into three social classes: a commercial elite that also assumed some responsibility for public order, a middle class of traders and artisans, and a vast urban proletariat. Those who were dubbed "outsiders" (in a city predominantly made up of immigrants!) constituted an underclass without moral claims on the city. Unfortunately, we do not know on what grounds this invidious distinction was made.

Flows of people into and out of Hankou continued throughout the first half of the twentieth century, as the city grew from a mere trading and transshipment center to an industrial metropolis. With revolution, civil war, and Japanese invasion, more and more people sought refuge in the city. This influx continued right on through the establishment of the People's Republic, even when the revolutionary government imposed its draconian household registration system in the mid-1950s for the purpose of constraining migration, especially to large cities.

ORIGINS AND CONSEQUENCES OF THE HOUSEHOLD REGISTRATION SYSTEM

Markets for commodities, including labor, do not exist in a Soviet-style economy where productive resources are allocated by the state and final products—food, housing, clothing, and so forth—are distributed through rationing. It is therefore not surprising that soon after gaining power, the communist regime took strong measures to allocate peasants and workers to specific work assignments and thus also to particular localities. Although Article 90 of the 1954 Constitution guaranteed citizens freedom of residence, a directive issued by the Ministry of the Interior and the Ministry of Labor that very same year set out to "control the blind influx of peasants into cities." The term *mangliu* (blind migrant) was widely used to describe rural migrants. As explained by Cheng and Selden (1994, 654), *mangliu* is a reverse homophone for *liumang*, meaning "hooligan," thus setting the tone for the whole debate. Henceforward, all population and labor flows from the countryside to cities would be decided by the state.

One of the reasons for this decree was planners' concern with the costs of urbanization, costs that in socialist ideology were regarded as unproductive and that, in the absence of a private sector, would all have to be borne by the state. To all intents and purposes, the People's Republic was a closed economy (especially after 1960, when China broke with the Soviet Union) and was thus extremely short of capital. Population was steadily increasing, and the production of grains sufficient to feed this growing population was a first priority. Even so, throughout the 1950s the newly formed state enterprises recruited rural labor in large numbers. And most of these workers brought their families with them. Central planners were deeply troubled by this trend. Cheng and Selden (1994) write:

> The 27 November 1957 *People's Daily* bemoaned the practice of workers bringing their families to the cities, thus driving up costs to the state in the form of housing, health care, food subsidies and urban infrastructure. The article noted that from 1950 to the end of 1956, about 150,000 rural people came to Beijing to look for employment and the original workers and residents brought another 200,000 dependents to the city. Zhang Qingwu estimated the cost of constructing urban housing required for the 2.5 million workers and their 5.5 million family members who migrated to the cities between 1953 and 1957 at 4.5 to 5.6 billion *yuan* or 450–700 *yuan* per person. This was 70–80 percent of China's total industrial

investment in 1956. And these sums exclude the cost of feeding, educating and providing health care and other benefits to these urban migrants. (661)

Having consolidated institutions of police-administrative control over the movement of population, on June 22, 1955, the State Council passed, and Premier Zhou Enlai endorsed, "The Directive Concerning Establishment of a Permanent System of Household Registration." This directive formally initiated a full-blown *hukou* system on the eve of China's collectivization (ibid., 655). Household registrations were issued in two forms: individually registered urban households received a nonagricultural *hukou,* but in the newly collectivized countryside, each cooperative received only a collective registration for its members. For all practical purposes, the cooperative (soon to be commune) was viewed as the relevant "household" of peasant families. To leave the collective (administrative village and township) for the city thus became all but impossible. Between 1961 and 1963, 26 million urban residents, many of whom had arrived there to work after 1949, were sent back to the countryside, resulting in a (temporary) net decline in the proportion of the urban population.

The new registration system was enforced with bureaucratic efficiency. In the case of mixed urban/rural couples, for example, the urban *hukou* holder could live in the city, but the other partner (and any of their offspring) had to continue to live in the countryside. By the same token, aging rural parents were unable to join their urban children. And because daily necessities were now rationed, beginning with grains, and ration coupons could only be redeemed in a person's official place of residence, it was next to impossible to survive for very long away from one's home.

This division of China's population into a privileged urban minority (about 17 percent) and an exploited rural majority (83 percent) in effect created a two-class society. To be rural was to be condemned to a life of hard work and poverty. To be urban was to have entitlements that included subsidized grains and fuel, housing, education, health care, and cultural opportunities—all of which were denied to the country's farmers. One's life chances were therefore a product of the household registration system. The logic behind this system was that China's urban-based industrial revolution could be accomplished only by extraction of a surplus from grain production and the mass mobilization of labor for capital projects. The country, it was argued, could not afford to urbanize by absorbing progressive numbers of people into cities. It lacked the resources for new housing and social infrastructure.

It was as if a Great Wall had been erected between urban and rural areas, writes Wang Feng (1997, 152). The *hukou* became the passport for traveling between as well as within the two sides of the wall. And in what it set out to do, the household registration system was relatively successful. According to Wang,

> With the help of the household registration system, China was able to achieve remarkable success in curtailing migration. . . . Non-agricultural product as the percent of national income grew from 52 percent in 1962 to 64 percent in 1978, while the proportion of urban population hardly changed at all. China experienced what may be called "industrialization without urbanization." Until 1982, the proportion of the population classified as urban only crept up very slowly, from 17 percent in 1970 to 21 percent. About 70 percent of those living in the urban [administered] areas (cities and towns) had non-agricultural status. In other words, of all population in China, only about 15 percent held an urban non-agricultural household status. (155)

In macro-economic terms, it was not a very efficient system.[1] And with the reforms beginning in late 1978, the restrictions on mobility were gradually—very gradually—relaxed. Young people who had been ruralized by the state were allowed to return to their native places in cities. Couples that had been divided because each partner held a different *hukou* were permitted to be reunited in the urban areas. And aging rural parents were allowed to join their urban offspring. More significantly, the countryside was de-collectivized, and agricultural production was now under a new "household responsibility system." This not only opened the door to a shift out of grains into higher value agricultural products such as fruits and small livestock, but was also the beginning of the helter-skelter rural industrialization described in the previous chapter. The first real reform of the household registration system, however, did not come until 1984, when for the first time the State Council permitted peasants to move into small towns (*jizhen*) below the level of county seat and, in doing so, allowed them to change their registration from an agricultural to a nonagricultural *hukou*.

This reform was so "successful" in releasing peasants from virtual bondage to their native villages that five years later, a panicking State Council established a system of quotas for the issue of nonagricultural *hukou* (Wang 1997, 159). By now, however, the genie was out of the bottle. In the meantime, as China progressively moved toward a market economy, even urban *hukou* had found a local market, starting at about 6,000 yuan. Anderson (2003) reports that in the coastal city of Quanzhou, investing in an urban apartment that cost upward of 100,000 yuan would buy three urban *hukou*. And the going price in Shanghai for a so-called blue-seal *hukou* was a cool 1 million yuan or purchase of 100 square meters of residential property priced for the foreign market (Wang 1997, 161).

An urban *hukou* might be "reaching for Heaven," but to migrate legally was a costly business. To get a job on the coast, a migrant had to obtain—usually for a price—various documents prior to leaving home: an identity card, the unmarried status certificate and/or birth certificate, the permit to work elsewhere, a good-conduct certificate from the local Public Security office, a family planning status for young women, and others. Migrants also needed to purchase a train or bus ticket and have enough money left over to cover expenses before receiving their first pay and also to buy a return ticket in case they didn't find a job. In the early 1990s, these expenses would have amounted to several hundred yuan (Chan 2002, 187n.54; Guldin 2001, 239). Clearly, it was far less trouble, and certainly less costly, to try one's luck without proper documentation and hope that one would not be picked up by Public Security and sent back home.

A second major reform of the household registration system came in late 2001, when the State Council allowed agricultural *hukou* holders to move to small cities and designated towns and, on condition that they had a stable job and a legal urban residence, exchange their old registration for a new nonagricultural work *hukou* (Wang 2002). The government was not yet prepared to lift residence restrictions altogether. Instead, it attempted to direct migrations to the tail end of the urban hierarchy (designated towns and cities of less than 200,000), though presumably as soon as towns were reclassified as administrative cities, and small cities grew to become middle-sized, either they would no longer be eligible migration targets or else, what is more likely, migrants would be permitted to move up one or two ratchets to a higher level in the urban hierarchy. This new regulation will make it more difficult to enforce continuing restrictions, since many designated towns and small cities actually fall within the administrative areas of large cities, and in the end, it will all be a matter of deciding how *urban* is to be defined.[2]

CHINA ON THE MOVE

Beginning in the mid-1980s, tens of millions of "peasants" (or more precisely, nonagricultural *hukou* holders) came flooding into coastal cities, their suburbs, and the rural and semi-rural areas surrounding them. How many there were, no one actually knows with any certainty. Jie and Taubmann (2002, 184) claim that a consensus has settled at around 60–80 million in the late 1990s, with about 50–60 million of them headed for urban areas, including the urban fringe. To the privileged urban residents, the presence of these strangers among them seemed like an invasion, and they saw their classic entitlements threatened by these uncouth "hordes" from the countryside. For their part, urban bureaucrats also saw migrants—many of whom failed to register with Public Security and whose presence was therefore regarded as illegal—as a threat. No one knew for sure how many there were or, for that matter, where they were living or even where they were coming from. And Chinese authorities—like authorities anywhere—dreaded the thought that here was a large population who were effectively beyond the state's reach, who in the perception of the bureaucracy were "out of control."

It was not even clear what to call these people who had abandoned their places of origin and were headed for who knew where. Dorothy Solinger, who has written one of the best books on the new mobility, uses terms that echo this uncertainty (1999). Some of them are her own, others are a direct translation from the Chinese. Most urban Chinese call them the floating population, or "floaters" for short. Others call them "blind drifters." More neutrally, urban bureaucrats refer to them as the "temporary population." Solinger herself refers to them variously as transients, sojourners, vagrants, wanderers. Most of these terms have a negative connotation for those who use them. People who don't belong to the local community are people one is not inclined to trust in the same way as long-term residents. And since one doesn't know them, it's easy to make up stories about them that quickly turn into stereotypes. Like European Gypsies, undocumented migrants to the United States from across the Mexican border, or the stock character of the Wandering Jew, they are seen as a rootless people. As the Chinese ditty has it (Solinger 1999, 256): "They live without any fixed abode, / Travel even without leaving a trace. / They conceal their identity, bury their names; / Between city and country they scatter apace."

Floaters in China today are the equivalent of the "dangerous classes" who were much feared in nineteenth-century Britain. They must therefore be closely watched and better yet, sent back to wherever they came from. And many, indeed, returned—some voluntarily, while others, rounded up by Public Security because they lacked the proper papers or a job, were forced to return home. In a recent year Shanghai repatriated some 100,000 "floaters"

(Unger 2002, 129), while the municipality of Beijing has periodically eradicated ethnic enclaves in advance of important international gatherings. The new mobility, it seems, is perceived to threaten not only the status quo of the urban class but public order as well. Solinger sums it up well:

> What peasants symbolized for city people, then, was the sense that what urbanites had considered their birthright, the urban public goods regime—according to which only they could deserve the benefits of privileged city living—was in transition, in decline. So as migrants became a metaphor for the markets they accompanied, their seeming assault on perquisites got much more attention than what was probably more important: their genuine contribution to the erosion of the administrative side of the planned economy and the model they provided of a new mode of economic activity. For as the transition to the market in the municipalities advanced, the mundane, daily activities of the floaters themselves—working at their trades, trading in the fairs, and struggling to survive—pushed the process onward. (Solinger 1999, 145–46)

It might be added that most urbanites rarely have personal encounters with new migrants. The migrants tend to live out of sight in urban fringe areas and beyond, or else they live on construction sites where they are an invisible blur, or in factories where they are tethered to their machines for twelve hours a day. So how would city people even begin to know about them? On the other hand, those who live in close proximity to migrant workers in such places as the suburban ethnic enclave of Zhejiangcun in Beijing (Zhang 2001) or on the outskirts of Quanzhou (Anderson 2003), tend to have a very different impression. They see migrants as neighbors with whom they do business by renting out rooms to them, or who have started a small local business of their own, are perhaps providing some local employment, and are welcome customers in local stores. Whether they have the proper household registration is a matter for Public Security to decide, not for neighbors.

TYPES OF MIGRANTS

There are several reasons why all estimates of the numbers of migrants are suspect:

1. They lack a clear-cut criterion of who is a migrant worker and who moves from one place to another for some other reason, such as to study, to conduct business, to make personal visits, and so forth.

2. They often count the same migrant more than once at different points in time.

3. They fail to distinguish among migrants in terms of both the length of time and distance of migration.

4. They are unable to make precise estimates of the number of unregistered migrants.

The same migrant, or migrant household, may move from place to place, in search of suitable work and reasonable living conditions. Some may at first migrate to towns near their native village before venturing into less familiar parts of the country. We may call them *serial* migrants. Others return to their native village only to set forth again at a later time. We may call them *repeat* migrants. A third group of migrants return home during harvest time or similar occasions that fall at regular intervals. We may call them *cyclical* migrants. A fourth type of migration occurs when, after a long period of absence, a migrant returns to his home town or village to start up a business of his own, or to retire. These may be called *return* migrants. And finally, there are those migrants who go to the city to remain there. They are part of the *permanent* migration.

In a 1993 study of the mobility status of peasant households in seven provinces, Hein Mallee discovered that a large number of households in his survey lived and worked in the same place, accounting for 47 percent of all households (N = 2,786) and 68 percent of all individuals (N = 6,735). Another 22 percent of households had at least one member who worked in a nearby township while the household continued to reside in the village. Only 3.1 percent of households had members who were absent from home for more than a year (1.6 percent of all individuals). Those who remained away from their village for between six and twelve months accounted for another 4.0 percent (2.2 percent of all individuals). And those absent for shorter periods were found in 4.5 percent of all households and accounted for 2.3 percent of all individuals (Mallee 1997, 285).

Although the precise percentages reported by Mallee are specific to this survey, the overall picture that emerges from this study is one of relative stability in rural areas, with surprisingly few migrants who stayed away from home for longer periods of time. The second significant finding is that even though a small majority of households had at least one of their members earning money outside the village, a little over one-fifth of all households had found work in the township where their village was located. They were thus short-distance migrants. Another fifth were merely commuting to work.

Guldin (2001, 227) cites an unpublished 1995 estimate made by Scott Rozelle, according to which one in ten farmers nationwide had found a job away from home. Whatever the accuracy of this estimate, one should not assume that all of these farmers had moved to distant locations. If Mallee's survey is generally indicative of the migrant situation throughout rural China, then of this one-tenth of the peasant population, many were actually working in townships near their native villages and very few of them might be considered "permanent" migrants. The majority would no doubt be considered either cyclical or repeat migrants. It is also possible that households would send more than one of their members to work outside the village, but in succession: as one daughter or son returned, another member would be sent out to seek their fortune.[3]

THE WORK MIGRANTS DO

It is generally accepted that the bulk of rural migrants end up doing work that is dangerous, dirty, and difficult: the notorious "Three Ds." This is partly because migrants tend to be less educated than urban *hukou* holders and generally lack the requisite skills for better paid work.[4] Increasingly, too, certain kinds of work are "reserved" for the growing number of legal urban residents who are unemployed. Many migrant workers work in small to medium-sized family enterprises. Others find jobs in jointly financed, larger factories producing primarily for export. Many men work in construction. Young women typically find work in garment industries and electronic assembly plants, but also as nursemaids in newly rich, middle-class households. Some of the more successful migrants succeed in opening up small businesses, such as hair dressing parlors or restaurants that cater mostly to other migrants, though a few may serve a more upscale market. The less fortunate become rag pickers and scrap collectors. A small number continue working in agriculture subcontracted to local farmers who have diversified their earnings to the point where they no longer need to work in the fields themselves (Solinger 1999, 206–38).

What will happen as China's economy becomes increasingly skill-intensive and as jobs for unskilled workers decline is anybody's guess. Some of this change—brought about, as Dorothy Solinger argues, by China's recent accession to the World Trade Organization (WTO)—may be turned into a soft landing for China's "surplus" of peasant laborers whose numbers are sometimes estimated at 200 million. This would occur as labor-intensive industries are shifted into the interior of the country, while coastal regions upgrade their jobs, reflecting China's new comparative advantage in the global economy (Solinger 2003).[5] But this regional displacement of labor-intensive jobs will probably not be enough to meet the needs of poor rural households, who will continue to move to larger coastal cities where they will earn money in the marginal trades and services of the informal economy.

CONDITIONS OF WORK FOR MIGRANTS

There is no question that in whatever job they do, migrant workers are either exploited or, if working for themselves, self-exploited. Working exceptionally long hours, they are paid—if at all—below the minimum wage. If they are young women, they can expect to be sexually abused. Beyond that, health conditions at work are often in violation, with workers having virtually no protection against potential hazards such as chemical fumes. If overcome by tiredness or sickness, they can be dismissed at a moment's notice. In other cases, their identity documents may be withheld to ensure that they serve out the length of their contract, which may be anywhere from one to three years. Many workers are housed in cramped dormitories, managed by the factory, that squeeze up to six women or men into a small room. And no matter what their grievances may be, they have no recourse to either labor unions or public authorities who, in any event, will nearly always back employers against workers. In short, young migrant workers, and especially women, are the cannon fodder of China's industrial revolution.

Anita Chan (2002) draws on the personal correspondence received by young women in a Shenzhen factory that burned to the ground in the early 1990s. Unable to escape because of bolted doors, barred windows, and blocked exits, eighty-seven women perished when a fire broke out at the Zhili Toy Company, a Hong Kong–based firm. Hundreds of letters they had received from friends and relatives, in many cases migrant workers themselves, were subsequently discovered among the charred remains, and a selection of these forms the basis of Chan's heartrending account. Many first-time migrants, it turns out, were uninformed about such "rights" as they had (pay scale, hours, and so forth), but even if they had known about ongoing practices, it probably wouldn't have mattered much, because there was no one who would speak up for them, and they were desperate for work. The legal workday in China is eight hours. Yet most young women found themselves working twelve-hour shifts, which were extended to eighteen hours when a rush job had to be done. Every couple of weeks they might get a day off. And pay was both below the legal minimum and irregular. "The pay was so sporadic," reports Chan, "that the workers commonly asked one another, 'Have you been paid yet?' The usual answer was, 'Not yet.' The norm was being owed wages instead of being paid. Consider this example: 'We have [finally] gotten our wages. Got December's pay on March 15. Got 140 yuan. I've sent 100 yuan home'" (Chan 2002, 167). For comparison, the minimum legal wage for Shenzhen was 280 yuan at the time; in Guangzhou city it was 230 yuan.

So long as there is an unlimited supply of unskilled labor, these conditions of work are likely to continue. They still prevailed in Quanzhou in 2002 (Anderson 2003). A decade after the letters from which Anita Chan quotes, the starting pay in Quanzhou's "rural industries" was around 300 yuan per month (= USD36), but even such a nominal amount may be withheld for some months to ensure that workers do not leave, regardless of how badly they are treated.[6] More experienced workers may receive up to twice this amount, but on an hourly basis that is still barely 2 yuan per hour, or about 24 yuan for a day's work (= USD2.85 for a twelve-hour day). Against this income, there are expenditures of at least 30–60 yuan per month for a bunk in a dormitory room with five other workers and of about 100 yuan for food, while renting a single room from a local villager might cost 200–300 yuan per month (Anderson 2003, 49–53). Clearly, an ordinary factory worker could not afford such a luxury.

Of course, not everyone is an unskilled apprentice worker in Quanzhou. In the city center, attractive young women are employed in beauty salons as hair washers (which includes a neck and back massage lasting about half an hour) for up to 1,000 yuan, while a senior hairdresser in a more established shop on Nanjun Road may earn more than 3,000 yuan. And some migrants also run their own businesses.[7]

Even so, most workers try desperately to save money, not only for the yearly trip back home over New Year—when "half of China" travels home, laden with presents and cash—but also to send regular remittances to families left behind. Guangdong villagers told Gregory Guldin that they received at least 100 yuan per month from relatives in delta factories, and more highly paid construction workers may send up to 300 yuan per month (Guldin 2001, 237). Given the hand-to-mouth existence of rural households in sending provinces, these amounts are not negligible. Solinger (1999) has attempted to assess aggregate amounts for two provinces:

> By the first half of the 1990s the most prevalent reports were of remittances in
> the billions, aggregated at the level of the province. For instance, the more than

five million Hunanese surplus rural laborers who found jobs outside the province brought home an income of about 5 billion yuan in 1994 [less than 1,000 yuan per worker, a not unreasonable amount]; according to one account, Anhui sent out the same number of workers and received as much as 7.5 billion back in 1993. If these figures are accurate, what Hunan's migrants contributed amounted to about 3 percent of gross domestic product (GDP) in the province for that year, and what Anhui's gave was 7 percent there. (190–91)

But migrant income is paid for in blood. The extraordinarily frugal lives of most rural migrants are well documented. Even so, figures such as these are at best "guesstimates" that will vary from year to year, or even season to season. Whatever the "true" amounts are, they are no doubt substantial at the provincial level and even more so at the level of the migrants' home communities. Helping to support their families is a major reason why people leave home.[8]

New dormitories for factory workers in Dong Mei village, Quanzhou, Fujian Province, 2003

MIGRANT ENCLAVES

Just as overseas migrants in large Western cities have tended to cluster upon arrival, forming a Chinatown, a Little Italy, a Little Saigon, and—as in Los Angeles—Koreatown, so many migrants in China's big cities sort themselves out according to their perceived ethnicity, their native villages and region (Jie and Taubmann 2002).⁹ They may all be "Chinese" or even "Han," terms that are not very useful to distinguish people by their "ethnicity" in China—that is, by their language, clothes, eating habits, and even religion.¹⁰ Ethnic enclaves are called "villages" (*cun*) and some are preceded by the name of the province from which migrants come. Thus Beijing has its Henancun, Anhuicun, Xinjiangcun, Zhejiangcun, and so forth, whose inhabitants think of themselves as *tongxiang* or compatriots ("homies") and stand ready to help and support each other in finding jobs, in battling the local authorities, in taking care of their own.

The term *village* is somewhat misleading, write Jie and Taubmann, "since it is not a natural village created by migrants, but a conglomeration of dwellings mostly located in the peri-urban zone. These 'villages' of several thousands or even tens of thousands of temporary residents might expand over four to five preexisting natural villages (*ziran xun*) or even a number of administrative villages (*xingzhengcun*)" (188). According to official figures for China as a whole, about 40 percent of the migrant population occupied rented quarters in 1997, 30 percent lived in company dormitories, and 17 percent lived on construction sites (187). These data are for registered migrants only. But in November 1995 only 40 percent of temporary migrants were registered with Public Security. The rest had disappeared into their "villages" where they remained invisible to the authorities.

Because most migrants are highly mobile, urban authorities are unable to monitor their comings and goings. Circular migration is common; many migrant workers return home during the harvest or spring festival, and during their absence most landlords rent out the vacated rooms to others without reporting to the responsible housing office. Besides, not a few local officials are open to bribery and tolerate illegal practices (186). As Li Zhang writes, referring to the frustrations of the local state in its inability to monitor migrant life down to the last detail, "no gaze is all-encompassing" (Zhang 2001, 212). This is something every migrant already knows, and of course it infuriates the bureaucracy.

Migrants' ability to elude the local authorities derives in part from the conflicting interests of different bureaucracies. While the city labor bureau

Street in informal settlement of migrants from Zhejiang Province in the suburbs of Beijing

may want full employment and will try to limit the number of migrant "outsiders," the commercial and industrial bureau will try to generate income and support migrant entrepreneurs. And local township and village governments, not to mention the indigenous population renting out rooms to migrants, who eat in their restaurants or work in their workshops, will be inclined to be more friendly toward the newcomers. Li Zhang, an anthropologist who studied one of the most famous of migrant villages in Beijing (Zhejiangcun) is not only aware of migrants' countervailing power with regard to authorities but also conscious of how their presence both reflects and acts upon the restructuring of urban space and the larger society.

> The migrants' emerging power is both conditioned by and derived from the migrants' spatial mobility and the production of their own space. What we have seen [in her telling of the story of Zhejiangcun] is a highly contested process in which existing socialist spaces (villages, factories, and other space-dominated sites) were transformed into different kinds of spaces more suitable for private economic practices and capital accumulation by migrant entrepreneurs. Because rural migrants in China are defined as outsiders and strangers in the cities and denied formal urban membership and substantive rights, their creation of new social space outside the regime of official planning has profound social and political implications. Such spatial transformations are not just about physical space, but are integral, dynamic aspects of the late-socialist transformations that will reshape the economic and social trajectory of Chinese society. (202–3)

The contest between the informal migrant economy and the local state continues. For example, in Beijing, because of the massive layoffs from large, state-owned enterprises, the municipal government urged unemployed urban workers to "learn from rural migrants" to be "on their own"—that is, to take up temporary work—as in construction or services, work traditionally rejected by most urbanites—or to create their own jobs, such as opening up small businesses. On the other hand, on October 1, 1999, the People's Republic of China celebrated its fiftieth anniversary by holding a grand ceremony in the capital. To prepare the capital for the commemoration of this event, the government mobilized another great clean-up campaign. This so-called beautification program proposed to tear down 2.6 million square meters of illegally built structures, most of which were temporary housing, stores, restaurants, and street markets established by migrants or shanties rented to migrants. In other words, the campaign set out to erase the very alternative spaces created by the migrants themselves (Zhang 2001, 210–11). Once the festivities were over, however, these same spaces were soon reoccupied as the ever resilient migrants returned to their "villages." The lesson from experiences of this kind is that migrants from the countryside are in the city to stay, and that the spatial transformation that enables them to survive is a process that can no longer be stopped.

RETURN MIGRATION

Little has been written about migrants returning from the city to their home communities, but this is becoming an increasingly important chapter in the history of China's migration. Some, of course, return as failures, but others are hailed as local heroes. Rachel Murphy writes about one of them. "Ouyang Xiafang, director of the Jinda Shiye Group Company in Yudu, is one example of a model returnee entrepreneur. . . . The Ouyang Complex, the tallest building in Yudu, incorporates a restaurant, shops, a hotel, and offices. It stands in the middle of the county town, metaphorically proclaiming the rise in the status of a lowly farmer: he earned his money as a labor contractor in Guangzhou and Xiamen, then invested in mines and factories at home" (Murphy 2002b, 234). Murphy conducted her research in two rural counties in Jiangxi Province, a relatively poor region bordering on Fujian, Zhejiang, and Guangdong Provinces.[11] She reports that according to official estimates in 1997, one-third of rural migrants from Sichuan, Hunan, and Jiangxi are returning home (230). Even more recently, the return flow of migrants to northern Jiangsu Province has been 25 percent greater than the reported outflow. As the cityward migration fever is dying down and first-hand knowledge about the realities facing rural migrants in coastal areas is spreading, expectations are readjusted and the rural-to-urban flow changes along with it.

But migrants bring more than their accounts of life in the mythical cities of the east. They bring new skills, know-how, and ways of life to what were only recently isolated and relatively self-contained "natural" villages. Assisted by local town and county governments, return migrants may start up small businesses, and one or another may entice a Hong Kong investor to enter into a partnership to produce furniture, clothing, shoes, or toys for export. In the late 1990s, according to Murphy (2002b), there were 1,450 returnee enterprises in Yudu County. The three largest of them had an annual output of 100 million yuan (231). As wage levels slowly rise on the coast, backcountry areas like Yudu County can still offer huge quantities of low-cost labor.

The local state is eager to encourage and promote returnee entrepreneurship through preferential policies, publicity campaigns, and personal overtures to successful migrants in coastal cities. Writes Murphy: "Spring Festival is an ideal occasion for local officials to remind those migrants who have prospered not to forget the home soil that has nourished them. From January to March newspapers carry stories of migrants who have donated money to rural infrastructure projects, or who have prospered by setting up businesses. Banners at rural bus stations greet returnees: 'Welcome Migrants to Come Home and Create Businesses'" (234–35). In the late 1990s county delegations visited urban destinations in an effort to persuade migrants to open businesses at home. These visits have yielded results: in Murphy's study, twelve out of twenty-seven large-scale manufacturing enterprises, four out of twenty-six small-scale manufacturing entities, and one out of five farming ventures were established as a result of official representation (235).

A particularly innovative initiative by local governments in Jiangxi was an effort to train migrants from their own region during their sojourn in eastern cities so that they might contribute more effectively to economic development at home. Evening and weekend courses for migrants range from basic numeracy and literacy classes to vocational training in car repair and electronics (236). According to township officials in Jiangxi, migrant money funds over half of local construction activity. In this way, economic growth is filtered back into the sending areas of migrants. It is perhaps a hopeful sign that the gross income inequalities created by Deng Xiaoping's policy of "letting some get rich first" will eventually be attenuated as a result of the attachment many, perhaps most Chinese have to their places of origin and their ancestral villages. Rachel Murphy, for one, is hopeful:

> Operating within local state corporatism, returnees are able to pursue their own goals, namely accumulating capital through independent means. Yet, in rural areas, problems with town infrastructure and government policy inhibit the realization of this goal. Through negotiation with the local state, returnees help to make the natal environment more conducive to business. This is illustrated by the actions of returnees and migrants in improving town infrastructure, salvaging ailing government enterprises, contesting the claims of officials on business resources, injecting capital into the local economy, expanding credit supplies, integrating the local markets into the national economy, and fostering rural-urban market linkages. (244)

MIGRANT PROSPECTS

Reliable, up-to-date statistics on migration streams are not yet available for China. It is therefore impossible to speak with any degree of confidence about the future of migration. The general long-term trend is toward successive increases in the proportion of urban population, but some significant part of urbanization in the demographic sense is a result of the reclassification of what were formerly "rural" areas.[12] Some qualitative observations may nevertheless give us a basis for a considered judgment.

As market signals, including the price for labor, become increasingly accepted as a legitimate basis for decision-making in the private, collective, and public sectors, *hukou* system restrictions on labor mobility are gradually vanishing. This is partly because of the large (and possibly growing) number of "undocumented" migrants who simply fail to register with Public Security—the state, as Li Zhang reminds us, is not omniscient—and partly because of the recent reform in the *hukou* system itself. An example of this is the 2001 decision by the State Council to allow "peasants" to move freely to designated towns and small cities—that is, cities with less than 200,000 population (Wang 2002). In 1999 China had 368 such cities and over 20,000 designated towns. These numbers suggest that at least some migrant flows will be diverted from the mega-cities on the coast toward centers closer to the home villages of migrants, thus resulting in a reduction of long-distance migration. The extent to which this policy will be successful, however, will depend on the ability of towns and small cities to accelerate their own economic growth and to create new jobs.

This may be difficult, but it is not impossible. Return migration, as Rachel Murphy's research has shown (Murphy 2002a; Murphy 2002b), is beginning to take place, leading to positive results for local economies. Moreover, the rising price of labor in coastal cities is beginning to force a shift in labor-intensive production, such as in garments, shoes, and toys, into the interior. At the same time, the growing autonomy of local governments frees their hand to adopt tried and proven methods of place promotion, ranging from tax incentives to the provision of economic infrastructure.[13] Innovative programs such as those reported by Murphy for Yudu County in Jiangxi Province, and those which have been widely noted in the public media, may be replicated elsewhere. And as the national system of transport and communication improves, it will open up regional and national markets, creating for the first time in China's history an integrated space economy whose potential for growth has as yet scarcely been plumbed. China's ancient archipelagic economy, with its implied requirement for regional self-reliance, has already passed into historical memory. Even though the present export orientation of its economy will undoubtedly continue for years to come, a growing share of economic growth is likely to be generated through an expansion of national markets.

This prospect for the multiplication of urban production centers throughout China is reinforced by the government's own recognition that the time has come to shift attention from coastal to interior regions and to avert the possibility that regional disparities will explode into massive social unrest (Shambaugh 2000). Recent five-year plans reflect this growing awareness of the importance of regional development.

So we conclude that urban migration in its multiple forms—permanent, seasonal, cyclical, serial, return—will continue. Coastal cities, however, will reduce their share of the total as urban centers in the interior start up their own phase of accelerated economic growth.

There remains, however, an invisible dimension of migration, which has been succinctly noted by Dorothy Solinger (1999). Migrants to cities, she observes, *are writing new rules of urban life*.

> In the transitional era when China was forsaking its socialist pattern, by the very act of sanctioning markets, its leadership was also involuntarily relinquishing its monopoly on the bestowal of the trappings of urban citizenship, insofar as these amounted to a share in the distribution of public goods and the right to membership in a community. The state was also thereby abandoning (if similarly unintentionally and surely unwillingly) its stranglehold over forms of association outside its own aegis. In short, because of their exclusion by the state institution of the *hukou*, combined with the workings of incipient markets, peasants in the cities—just by their presence alone—were participating in writing new rules of urban life. (274–75)

It is to these "new rules" that we now turn.

5. Expanding Spaces of Personal Autonomy

This chapter is about everyday life in China's large cities. Its focus is on the life of those who are considered official residents—urban *hukou* holders—thus bypassing the very different experiences of rural migrants in these cities, whose story was told in chapter 4. But even a highly selective account of everyday life cannot dispense with theoretical underpinnings. Personal autonomy is about the ability to make choices, from small ones, such as "Shall I go to the movies this evening or visit my mother who lives across town?" to major life-choices, such as whether to get married or divorced. Because such choices usually involve others as well as oneself, we resort to a concept of the *private sphere*, which is a domain of individuals, households, and families where choice can be exercised without direct intervention, guidance, or approval by the state. To invoke a term such as "private," however, is already to imply the existence of a more inclusive term, a *public sphere*, which together with the private defines a political space. Although in China political space remains the exclusive domain of the Communist Party, the matter cannot rest there—at least for a Western observer—because it raises important questions that are a central concern of our own political life: the meaning of citizenship, political choice, citizen rights, public participation, urban social movements, civil society. The mere mention of a public sphere, therefore, takes us to the heart of ongoing debates among China scholars in the West. Are our concepts about citizenship relevant to China? What are the indigenous theories or philosophical concepts that define the political for China yesterday, today, and perhaps tomorrow? Questions such as these go beyond what this chapter proposes to do. Even so, we cannot avoid them altogether and will return to them in the final pages.

In his doctoral dissertation of 1962, Jürgen Habermas cites the distinguished Austro-American economist Joseph Schumpeter to the effect "that the old forms that harnessed the whole person into systems of supraindividual purpose had died and that each family's individual economy had become the center of its existence, that therewith a private sphere was born as a distinguishable entity in contrast to the public" (Habermas 1989, 19). This sentence, written in 1918 at the end of World War I, might well serve as the motto for the present chapter. Schumpeter had in mind the collapse of the "feudal" order in Western Europe and the emergence during the nineteenth century of a bourgeoisie whose concerns were, at least in some respects, intensely private. And yet, despite its historical specificity, Schumpeter's succinct statement seems equally applicable to the post-Mao era in China.[1] For forty years the supra-individual system of revolutionary communism had subsumed anything that might still be called "private" until there was nothing left that was not also of concern to the party-state. Neighbors kept a sharp eye on each other's personal affairs, and the *danwei* to which they belonged saw its obligation to act *in loco parentis*. The public sphere—the concern with the common good—was internalized by the Communist Party, where it was articulated through the principle of hierarchy whose summit was Mao himself.

With the reform period, all this changed—or, more accurately, some of it changed, as the state began to back off from its insane attempt to control virtually every aspect of everyday life. The result was an astonishing expansion of the personal space of autonomous choice.[2] In addition to the exceptionally high rates of economic growth that have prevailed so far and have brought into being an urban "moneyed class" (a proportionately small but rapidly growing segment of the population), two other changes have occurred that have set the pace for a more autonomous life: the remarkable growth of unstructured "free" time, and an extraordinarily successful and sustained period of urban residential construction.[3] Following a brief discussion of these parameters, and some related examples of what I call the new sphere of intimacy and Chinese consumerism, I proceed to a discussion of the political space in which personal autonomy is embedded and the prospects of redrawing this space according to the Chinese saying, "small government, big society." I conclude by examining the idea of local citizenship and the related concept of citizen rights, and their pertinence to research on city life in China, using the work of Dorothy Solinger (1999) as a critical text.

THE USES OF DISPOSABLE LEISURE TIME

There are two parameters for the emergence of a private sphere in China: disposable leisure and a home of one's own. According to Shaoguang Wang, the control of leisure time can be achieved in one or more of three ways: regulating the disposable amount of leisure, regulating the forms of leisure, and regulating the contents of leisure. Mao's regime undertook all three of these (Wang 1995, 152). Until the late 1970s China was a thoroughly regimented society. The individual had been absorbed into the collective, and private time had all but disappeared. During episodes such as the Great Leap Forward (1958–61) and spurred on by eager cadres, peasants and workers drove themselves to exhaustion. During the height of the Cultural Revolution (1966–69), although bureaucratic regimentation broke down, urban residents were so terrorized by Red Guards and others that the concept of private leisure time lost its meaning altogether. People's lives were consumed by fear. Yet even in more normal times, the work unit (*danwei*) was the perfect institution for regimenting life during after-work hours. To begin with, *danwei* cadres often required overtime under the guise of volunteering labor, thus diminishing already scarce leisure. And even when not actually working, people could not call their time their own. Attendance at political study meetings was compulsory, team sports were favored over individual forms of recreation, and propaganda movies were shown to groups regardless of personal preference. It was a situation of enforced togetherness. Those who failed to participate in officially organized leisure activities risked being criticized for "cutting themselves off from the masses" and "lacking collective spirit" (153).

Under the best of conditions, disposable leisure time (after accounting for work and physiological needs) was pitifully small. Time-budget studies are unavailable for the period before 1980, but in that year, at the onset of the reforms, free time was benchmarked at two hours and twenty-one minutes per day. A mere eleven years later, it had already more than doubled (158).[4] Moreover, leisure time was no longer being mobilized by work units, or otherwise prescribed; under market socialism, one's leisure time was to be one's own.

Not surprisingly, much of the newly won time was spent watching television. By the end of the 1980s over 90 percent of urban households owned at least one television set. But there were other uses of unstructured time as well: thousands of hobby associations, from stamp collecting to breeding fish and admiring songbirds and crickets, sprang up throughout the country. Millions of readers eagerly snapped up the skyrocketing numbers of publications (newspapers, journals, and books). And wave after wave of new enthusiasms swept across China, such as *qigong* fever, tourism fever, keeping-fit fever, and dressmaking fever, as people indulged their new freedom (164–65). The work unit had given way to the apartment house, and one's home became a major site for leisure pursuits.

A HOME OF ONE'S OWN

The second parameter that made possible the impressive gains in personal autonomy was the boom in urban residential construction. "By 1995, more than half of all residential units [in urban China] were less than 16 years old . . . and average per capita living space was more than twice that of 1979," writes Deborah Davis (2002, 244).[5]

Shanghai followed these national trends. In the late 1970s most of Shanghai's 6 million urban residents lived in crowded apartments with few amenities. A majority shared bathrooms and kitchens with neighbors, and many used public latrines. Three-generation households were typical. Even married couples that lived independently of their parents or in-laws rarely had the luxury of a private bedroom separate from their children. In the entire metropolis only five buildings exceeded twenty floors.

New commodity housing in Beijing suburb, 1999

The changes made in this built environment after 1978 were mind-boggling. Between 1979 and 1989, 830,000 households occupied new or renovated apartments, and between 1992 and 1996 another 800,000 moved. More than 4.5 million people changed address, and average space per capita doubled, in most cases a move guaranteeing a higher material standard of living. By the late 1990s the norm for new construction was a three-room apartment looking out over a skyline punctuated with high-rise towers in diverse international styles. (244–45)[6]

More freely disposable time and a booming urban housing market together created the conditions for an expansion of the spaces of personal autonomy. I will report on two of these, under the headings of the new intimacy of life and the reemergence of the private sphere.

THE NEW INTIMACY OF LIFE

Over the past twenty-odd years the increases in disposable income, free time, and individually owned homes for small urban families have contributed to the recovery of a sphere of intimacy that had seemingly been lost during the period of collectivization. To illustrate this I will focus on two very different aspects: the desire for spiritual healing, and the heartbreaking stories of people whose personal relations had fallen on hard times and who were seeking counsel through anonymous telephone hotlines in Shanghai.

Here, first, is a Beijing story about the search for illumination and inner balance through the practice of *qigong*.[7]

In the early dawn at the Temple of Heaven Park about twenty practitioners can be observed at the stone altar in various states of *qi* meditation. Some sit in lotus position while others stand to concentrate on their breathing or lie on the stone in a trance. Nearby thirty other practitioners dance beneath trees or consult with one another on the best forms of practice, masters, and daily regimes. A few individuals communicate by speaking in tongues. They all appear to be ordinary people whom one might encounter throughout the day—storekeepers, street sweepers, free-market merchants, students, nannies. While *qigong* practitioners are visibly situated in public parks, their alternative states of consciousness imply a withdrawal from the confines of the city and the state.... *Qigong* practitioners rewrite their identity through healing practices in search of personal balance rather than state order. (Chen 1995, 360–61)

Throughout China, an estimated 200 million urbanites were practicing some sort of *qigong* during the early 1990s (ibid., 347). Nancy Chen interprets this flourishing of spiritualism as a response to psychological dislocation. "In place of urban anomie, there is a search for balance in one's life. Exercises in imagination and healing link one's body to the cosmos as an alternative to the alienation of life in the modern metropolis. . . . The spaces created through *qigong* reflect intimate relations among practice, body, and landscape and imply alternative mentalities outside the prescribed order of the state" (348).

To move now from the spiritual to the intensely personal realm, I will briefly recount what Kathleen Erwin (2000) discovered in her study of Shanghai advice hotlines. The first such hotlines were established in Tianjin and Beijing in 1989, and before long, they were all the rage throughout urban China. By the mid-1990s Shanghai could boast of more than twenty counseling hotlines, including call-in shows at Orient Radio, which had established its competitive niche by making them the basis for most of its programming. Programs dealing with questions of love, marriage, and sexuality that were

Village temple with new development under construction in Dong Mei village, Quanzhou, Fujian Province, 2003

broadcast until late into the night proved the most popular. A year after Orient Radio had gone on the air, its four phone lines were constantly busy, receiving up to forty-eight hundred calls per minute at peak times. One of the most popular of these shows, starting around midnight and dealing mostly with questions of unrequited love, extramarital affairs, and other romantic or familial problems, was called *Your Partner till Dawn* (157).

The media were new—the increasingly ubiquitous telephone (especially cellular phones) and call-in radio—and the problems people channeled through them had always been taboo subjects. People might whisper about them to their closest friend, but the idea of sharing their troubles with hundreds of thousands of listeners on talk-show radio was a thrilling new experience. Men mostly talked about sexual matters, such as the failure of their girlfriends or wives to respond to their overtures, and even about homosexuality and AIDS; women spoke of their worries concerning infidelity, divorce, child-rearing problems, personal relationships with in-laws, and sexual harassment by factory bosses. Particularly for women, the advice hotline was a way of breaking out—if only temporarily—of the emotionally stifling, extended family network with its multiple obligations and a work environment that was still very much constructed along patriarchal lines. Erwin (2000) comments that

> a common thread throughout these calls was the problem of striking a balance between newfound pleasures, freedoms, and material comforts and responsibility for family relations and marital stability. Family obligations, mate choice, sexuality, and divorce were viewed as common predicaments of modern life that posed a challenge to cultural wisdom and traditional values. That is, what was being negotiated in these calls were the gender roles and sexual expectations of modern men and women whose lives were structured not only by new economic and political reality but also by cultural constraints imposed by notions of Chinese tradition. (159)

The advice hotline is a way for women to claim new rights within the system of patriarchy, and for both men and women to learn what it means to be modern, in the context of present-day China. Despite the intimate and forbidden nature of the topics aired, hotlines have contributed to a vibrant public interest in family and sexual matters. Spawned by the new discourse, publications that address these questions, including sexual education, have flooded bookstores throughout China's cities.

THE REEMERGENCE OF THE PRIVATE SPHERE: LEARNING TO CONSUME

With the uniform, antlike character of "the masses" rapidly transmuting into individuals, with millions of urban households acquiring property in the form of a new home, and (of all things!) cheered on by the state to become more active consumers, it is small wonder that the young and educated, and even some of the older and less educated, are learning to become consumers.[8] True, associations in defense of consumer rights have been organized from above, but they accomplish their work all the same (Hooper 2000).[9] State support explains the wide coverage given to consumer grievances on television and the new opportunities provided by the Internet for public debate on consumer issues.[10] In 1996 the consumer affairs program *Focus* on national television claimed to be reaching an audience of 200 million (104). And the director of international crisis management for Edelman Publications, the world's largest public relations firm, warned clients: "[China's] consumers are finding their voice. . . . Business in China can now be impacted by interest groups in the same way as the rest of the world" (92). This comment, Hooper writes, was provoked "by growing protests against shoddy and fake consumer products, the expanding role of consumer associations, the consumer protection legislation of 1994, and subsequent claims against manufacturers, including foreign companies. According to a national survey in December 1997, consumer protection was the dominant legal concern of the urban population, cited by 29 per cent of the respondents, ahead of labor protection (25.5 per cent) and the criminal law (19.1 per cent). Environmental protection scored a mere 1.8 percent" (92). Apparently, consumer complaints are taken seriously. The China Consumer Association, a quango (quasi-official nongovernmental organization), reports that it handled 667,000 complaints in 1998 and claims a successful record, an average of well over 90 percent, in obtaining compensation (113). The volume of complaints has undoubtedly gone up considerably since then.

SMALL GOVERNMENT, BIG SOCIETY: RESHAPING RELATIONS BETWEEN STATE AND SELF

The foregoing snapshots of expanding personal autonomy in matters of everyday life may not seem much to a Western reader, accustomed to these liberties.[11] Such developments are precious only to those who until recently never enjoyed them. If someone wants to get married in Canada, they get married. They don't even have to consult their parents. In China, on the other hand, at least until October 1, 2003, a betrothed couple had to obtain permission to marry from their work unit or neighborhood committee. Wang Zhenyu, an expert on marriage at the Chinese Academy of Social Sciences, calls the lifting of this restriction "a revolution" (*Far Eastern Economic Review* 2003b, 30). In another easing of restrictions, migrant workers can no longer be detained and deported from cities for failing to carry the proper permits and identification (ibid.). But the Chinese party-state has not granted new rights to individuals; it has merely eased off in some areas of micro-managing people's lives. And whenever it wishes to do so, it can reimpose controls.

The question of politically guaranteed rights, and especially citizen rights, raises deeper questions about the role of civil society, the public sphere, and social movements in the development of rights, all of which are concepts in political philosophy. Western theorists, for example, are likely to argue that "rights" have to be successfully claimed and defended against a state reluctant to grant them. Moreover, the enforcement of rights demands judicial institutions free from political control to which ordinary people can have recourse when their rights are being infringed. Such institutions do not exist in China at the present time.

The Chinese approach to enlarging the sphere of personal autonomy has taken another course. Long before the tragic events that unfolded on Tiananmen Square in June 1989, a young research fellow in the Chinese Academy of Social Sciences (CASS) developed some ideas that could be summed up in the catchy phrase, "small government, big society." His ideas bore an uncanny relation to some Western writings on "civil society." But rather than being labeled as a "dissident" and packed off to a labor camp for reeducation, Liao Xun in 1987 was appointed to a CASS working group that was charged with developing a blueprint for the economic, political, and social restructuring of Hainan, a large island in tropical China that was about to be designated a province and a special economic zone (Brødsgaard 1998).[12] "Liao Xun's ideas on 'small government, big society,'" writes Brødsgaard, "constitute the first major effort by a Chinese intellectual and scholar working within the system to elaborate a fundamentally reformed political system. . . . If fully implemented, [the reforms] will create the foundation of a new kind of civil society that has been so vigorously researched and discussed in the China field since 1989. However, it will be a kind of civil society implemented from above and not from below" (189–90).

Liao's principal argument is that the state must be streamlined to cure its "bureaucratic sickness." In the past, bureaucratic reforms failed to work because social organizations were not ready to assume the functions that had formerly been handled by the bloated state bureaucracy. "If you want to reduce government functions," writes Liao, "you must expand the functions of society. If Hainan is to cure the root of the bureaucratic sickness, it will be necessary to fundamentally change the old system where the individual depends on the enterprise and the enterprise depends on the state, and instead bring forth the pluralistic interests of society" (ibid., 193). Citizens should have the right to freely choose not only what they wish to obtain in a free market, but also their education or occupation; to decide whether they will participate in or withdraw from any enterprise, no matter what the ownership form, and to decide whether to open an individual or private enterprise (194). In general, comments Brødsgaard, "the new system . . . requires that government and society establish a brand-new relationship. It also requires that the organs of local power in Hainan province, e.g., the Provincial People's Congress, truly reflects the plurality of interests in Hainan. A step in this direction would be to introduce path-breaking direct elections" (197).

Liao Xun, the would-be democratic reformer, was eventually appointed vice director of a think-tank in Haikou, the capital of the new province, where, among other activities, he published a twice-weekly, front-page column in a leading newspaper, commenting on the local reform process. In typically Chinese fashion, his slogan, "small government, big society," communicates a desired direction of change in more down-to-earth language than the elusive and contested notion of a civil society. More important, his programmatic suggestions for reform were aligned with ongoing trends in China, which some commentators, perhaps overdramatically, have referred to as the "retreat of the state." This may explain why the central government allowed Hainan to proceed with its radical program of reforms as a learning experiment in one small and isolated corner of China.[13]

At this time, it is not clear whether the Hainan experiment will eventually serve as a model for the rest of the country, and with what consequences. It also leaves unanswered the question concerning the proper role of government. In his newspaper columns, Liao carefully sidesteps the political questions that are implied, but never spelled out, in his catchy slogan. But the impression one gains is that, attractive as it is, the slogan tends to be interpreted by the government in a special way: "small government," yes; but at least for now, "big society" is best read as "big markets."[14]

A CHINESE CIVIL SOCIETY?

In the wake of the events of June 1989, scholars began to debate the prospects for a more democratic China.[15] Most of these contributions take off from the early work of Jürgen Habermas (1989) and his concept of a public sphere as the implicit counterpart of the private sphere. "The economic activity that had become private had to be oriented toward a commodity market that had expanded under public direction and supervision: the economic conditions under which this activity now took place lay outside the confines of the single household; for the first time, they were of general interest" (19). Economic and social affairs during the nineteenth century became a matter of public interest in Western Europe and continue to be so right up to the present, but in China, what is of public or, more accurately perhaps, of common interest remains the exclusive domain of the Communist Party. A public sphere in the Western sense has therefore not appeared in China, and this has precluded the appearance of a civil society in the political sense, as a sphere of action beyond the reach of the state.

This is not the place to enter into a detailed philosophical debate over these issues. Instead, I would like to draw attention to Philip Huang's concluding essay to a symposium on public sphere and civil society, which appeared about a decade ago in *Modern China* (Huang 1993). Huang argues against the binary conception of state vs. individual in Habermas's treatment and in its place proposes a "third realm" of intermediary institutions as a focus for future research. In this he follows in the footsteps of Alexis de Tocqueville and others who have identified civil society with institutions that mediate between state and individual (de Tocqueville 1969; Friedmann 1998a).[16] In Huang's view, such a conception would prevent any tendency to reduce "third space" organizations to the realm of either state or society. He writes: "We would begin by acknowledging the simultaneous influence of both in a third space. . . . We would begin to see it as something with distinct characteristics and a logic of its own over and above the influences of state and society" (1993, 225).

Huang's suggestion has considerable merit. It avoids the difficulty of trying to make value-laden (and contested) Western concepts fit Chinese realities, while keeping social processes of change clearly in view. Even in the West, organized civil society exists mostly for itself, in pursuit of its particularistic interests, from music to sports, from community service to the promotion of public festivals. At the same time, the capacity for self-organization in China is every bit as developed as it is in many Western countries. The difference is that the state in China is omnipresent, while in the West it is largely absent from the direct control and oversight of civil organizations.

In one of the best studies of Chinese "intermediate" organizations, Gordon White distinguishes four strata:

A *"caged" stratum* of mass organizations (such as the All-China Federation of Trade Unions)

An *incorporated stratum* of officially recognized social organizations (business, trade, professional, academic, sports, recreational, and cultural), of which by late 1993 there were already 1,460 at the national, 19,600 at the provincial, and 160,000 at the county level

An *interstitial stratum* of mostly local organizations that while officially registered, and despite some degree of state supervision, are more or less free to pursue their interests without direct interference from above

A *suppressed stratum* that includes a wide variety of political and social organizations as well as secret societies and other criminal organizations. (White 1996, 196–222; see also the more thoroughly documented study by White, Howell, and Shang 1996)

Most would agree that the last of these categories should be excluded as forms of "civic" organizations. Some would undoubtedly also wish to exclude the "caged" stratum from further consideration as "intermediate" institutions. But without detailed inquiry, who is to say that China's state-sponsored mass organizations are forever locked into their role of pandering to party directives? Consider, for example, Joseph Cheng's (2000) observations on the All-China Federation of Trade Unions:

The Party wants to strengthen its influence among workers. There is a serious concern that with market reforms, separation of state from enterprises, emphasis on profits, etc., the Party faces a considerable erosion of its previous role among workers. Beginning from the early 1990s, the Party has openly demanded for the establishment of Party organs and official trade union branches in foreign-owned enterprises and joint ventures. Yet as Kevin Jiang has observed, under pressure from the workers and for their own self-interest, the All-China Federation of Trade Unions (ACFTU) "has sought to represent workers' interests and to attain organizational autonomy by confronting a paternalistic, authoritarian political structure." The ACFTU has been moving cautiously given the current political constraints, and Jiang believes that it should not be seen as "conservative" but "pragmatic." (20)

Cheng extends his nuanced analysis of the ACFTU to other mass organizations:

> Gradually various mass organizations in China will be hard-pressed by their membership to articulate their interests and seek greater autonomy from Party control. There is no intention to confront the Party and state authorities concerned; the approach is usually low-key, patient and pragmatic. The Party and state authorities are persuaded that their vital interests are not threatened, that they will retain ultimate control, but in order to improve Party-mass relations, it will be better for the Party to reduce its presence and interference in the daily affairs of the mass organizations. . . .
>
> The ultimate test for China's mass organizations will be financial self-sufficiency. . . . [I]ncreasingly they will have to find means of expanding their incomes through charging fees for their services and establishing enterprises of their own. State subsidies will be reduced and they will probably come as lump sums, while mass organizations will have to pay salaries for their staff members from their budgets. Under such circumstances, mass organizations will have to streamline their organizations. (ibid.)

If we now combine White's typology with Cheng's observations on the so-called caged stratum of intermediate organizations, it would be reasonable to conclude that the rapidly expanding incorporated and interstitial strata not only would tend to be considerably more autonomous from control by the party-state than the official mass organizations, but also would continue to move in the direction of even greater autonomy, and thus toward a more Western form of civil society acting for itself.

Nevertheless, it is important to remind ourselves that the pursuit of political aims by social movements, political parties, and the like is strictly forbidden, and any attempt to do so will be quickly nipped in the bud. This raises a question about the meaning of citizenship and associated rights in China.

ON LOCAL CITIZENSHIP AND CITIZEN RIGHTS

Citizenship has been the subject of two recent books: Merle Goldman and Elizabeth Perry's *Changing Meanings of Citizenship in Modern China* (2002) and

Dorothy J. Solinger's *Contesting Citizenship in Urban China* (1999). The first of these is a collection of essays that ranges widely over many facets of what the editors are careful to note is their primary interest in *political* citizenship — that is, demands for greater participation and inclusion in the polity by various elements of the population. Their volume covers such diverse topics as village elections, the National People's Congress, the PRC Constitution of 1982 as amended, ethnicity and gender, legal institutions, public oratory, and the Democracy Wall Movement in the post-Mao era. Important as these contributions undoubtedly are, they are only tangentially related to the topic of this chapter.

Dorothy Solinger's volume is a different matter. She uses *citizenship* in the specific sense of what Henri Lefebvre, the French Marxist philosopher of urban life, once called "the right to the city" (Lefebvre 1968) and what Douglass and Friedmann (1998) in their collective volume called "cities for citizens." Although they point to a generally democratic and egalitarian conception of urban life, both of these phrases are open to interpretation. Solinger's book is about rural-urban migration, and she is severely critical of the *hukou* system, which, in her view, has created a two-class society consisting of those who are entitled to certain privileges of urban life and those who are not.

> In China the sudden mixture of a multitude of peasant migrants with established urbanites in cities in the transition to a market economy offers researchers an important opportunity: the chance to speculate about how markets affect citizenship and precisely because of the incursion of markets—where the state's former capacity to determine definitively both the allocation of the goods of daily life and the roster of membership in the urban community is clearly waning. With what logic do markets affect this process? And what is the content of citizenship—the privileges of membership—under these circumstances; just who qualifies to receive them? (Solinger 1999, 278)

Solinger's book addresses these issues. At the same time, she is aware that the *hukou* system of population control is itself weakening and that more and more urban entitlements are being articulated through the market. Under these conditions, it is no longer clear what the "right to the city" might mean in actual practice. Does it include the right to be homeless? The right to work? The right to a decent meal? The right to take to the street and protest exploitation, corruption, displacement, or lack of public services? The right to voice one's opinions? The right to be free from police harassment?

The belief that citizenship somehow confers individual rights (whatever they may be) is a distinctly Western and more specifically American conception. Although political theorists remind us that rights must be balanced by duties, the roster of citizen duties in a Western-style democracy is actually quite short: to live within the law, to pay taxes, and perhaps to perform jury service (and in some cases military service) when called upon. In China, the emphasis is the reverse of this: in a society still permeated by a Confucian ethos, where one's identity, based on the patriarchal model of the family, is determined by one's relations to specific others, obligations always come first, and privileges (rights?) second. Roger V. Des Forges (1997, 95) refers to an essay by R. P. Peerenboom (1993) in which the latter claims to have induced a Chinese theory of rights that holds rights to be contingent on time and place, communitarian in theory and practice, ethically inspirational, socially relational, and with an emphasis on mediation over confrontation and on economic benefits over political privileges. Des Forges is careful to point out, however, that the Chinese Constitution, though it mentions certain guarantees in principle, also assigns duties toward family members and fellow citizens as well as toward the state. Assuming that Peerenboom's theory of rights with, as he calls it, "Chinese characteristics" has some degree of validity, it is far from being a theory of universal entitlements, such as the phrase "citizen rights" would seem to suggest. It is also clear that obligations, particularly toward the state but also toward family members and community, are a pronounced feature of a Chinese theory of rights. One might add that whereas citizens in Western democracies have recourse to an independent system of courts when they believe that their rights are being violated, such a system of courts does not exist in China. In China, certain economic rights may be guaranteed by the Constitution, but ordinary citizens have little chance to press for their enforcement. In the end, Chinese citizens are still the subjects of the party-state.

In transitional China, a private sphere has been emerging from Maoist totalitarian rule that has materially expanded the sphere of individual choice in many aspects of life. As the economy grew helter-skelter during the 1980s and 1990s, especially along the coast, more and more people could buy their way into what they imagined to be the good life. The drab uniformity of collective life was considerably eased, and personal advancement was treasured above conformity to rules. Money became the universal solvent, and this necessarily led to new forms of social stratification at the same time as enforced

Maoist austerity yielded to the temptations of personal greed. This matter was of concern to the political leadership in Beijing, but repeated anticorruption campaigns have had relatively little effect on the overall level of corruption, which has remained high. In China, no less than in the West, the private sphere is necessarily embedded within a public or political sphere, and in both world regions, public and private are inevitably in tension. But in China, the Communist Party has preempted the public sphere, whereas in Europe, North America, and a few other regions, it is the sphere of democratic politics. Popular participation in politics falls short of what many theorists hold out as the ideal of the *polis,* though even in ancient Greece, which still provides us with a template for judging the forms and depths of democratic life, active citizenship was limited to the adult free male population and thus to only a minority.[17] But alongside electoral politics, from which many people in the West are profoundly alienated, many countries have a free-spirited politics fueled by fractions of organized civil society capable of mobilizing public opinion around issues of common concern and agitating for legislative changes and new citizen rights. This is the politics of social movements.

Such a politics does not exist in China where, except for rural villages, there is no electoral politics at all, and where political advocacy, even within the Communist Party, is narrowly constrained by the principle of hierarchy. The Chinese political system remains, at least from a Western perspective, strangely lopsided in that it lacks a counterpart to the private sphere—that is, a sphere of politics that is open to all.

For most Chinese today, a "civil society" means little more than the pursuit, in association with others, of their material interests and personal hobbies. Intermediate associations, however—Philip Huang's "third realm"—are proliferating at a breathtaking pace and in practice are becoming increasingly autonomous from state tutelage. The urban apartment with its new conveniences—TV, the Internet, refrigerator, air conditioning—is becoming a center of family life free from the snooping and constant supervision of party watchdogs under the *danwei* system, and the incessant struggle meetings and other collective activities that used to be thought of as the proper uses of leisure time under the Maoist regime. Intellectual life, too, is once again flourishing in urban China, with thousands of new publications appearing in bookshops and on newsstands. So long as the party-state itself is not directly challenged, an ever-widening range of opinions and interest articulations can be publicly discussed.

In the following chapter, I turn to the related matter of governance in the management of cities. Chinese cities are administrative, not corporate, entities, and their authorities are appointed rather than elected. Moreover, most cities also have authority over surrounding rural counties, which in the size of their population may surpass by many times that of the central city. China, therefore, has a unified form of city-regional governance that for some Western observers would be a source of envy. The story of local governance in China has not yet been written, and what follows has had to be cobbled together from different sources that cover only a very small number of cities. Diversity in China is great, and physical restructuring is continuing apace. How to manage all this, maintaining an appearance of orderliness while building livable cities, continues to be a formidable challenge.

6. The Governance of City-Building

The governance of city-building is the political dimension of urbanization whose multiple meanings we are exploring in this book. Like the city itself, urban governance is not immutable, but is in a constant state of adaptation and change. As the structures and processes by which citizens are ruled in any given polity, governance may be judged as more or less effective, more or less corrupt, more or less just. In contrast with the other dimensions of urbanization, however, it cannot be discussed outside of a normative framework that is a model either of the "good city" or of good governance itself (Friedmann 2002).

Unfortunately, there are no such models directly applicable to China, whose open cities were never thought of as standing apart from the countryside—or as the famous saying went in medieval Europe, "city air sets one free." Chinese cities were never corporate entities with their own legislative bodies, and never became cradles of democracy.[1] Nor are there current models of "good governance" outside the classical models of Confucian virtue (the cultivation of character on the part of the ruler and those who served him) and the Legalist principle of hierarchy.[2] Although Confucians argued for the merits of a bureaucracy steeped in the classics, and the pre-Han Legalists believed in exemplary laws and norms of conduct, statecraft in practice was considered to be merely a matter of administrative technique rather than of governance in a broader, more value-laden sense. In the end, throughout China's millennial history, there were only subjects of the imperial presence himself, never citizens with specific rights and obligations.[3]

The absence of a normative discourse on these questions does not mean, however, that cities in China were not governed, or that people lacked a sense of good governance in their unreflected notions of effectiveness and fairness. But in an era of mega-city regions and what Marx once referred to as "primitive accumulation," such notions are insufficient to ensure good governance.[4] Nor will Confucian virtue and the principle of hierarchy alone solve problems of combining hyper-rapid urban expansion with widely accepted norms of efficiency, livability, and sustainability.

Important though they are, these questions cannot be dealt with here at length. In a party-state that still deals with its citizens as passive subjects, a normative discourse on the principles of good governance would open up a range of issues that lie outside the scope of this chapter. In the following pages, I will explore the governance of cities in China, particularly with regard to urban land management, housing, and planning. In the first half, I explore the historical practices of governance in imperial, republican, and revolutionary China. Deeply embedded in Chinese society, these traditions linger on and have shaped the city during the past quarter-century of reforms. The remainder of the chapter briefly comments on the present institutional structure of local governance and asks the question of what happens when cities cease to be mere assemblies of buildings and set out to become entrepreneurial. Finally, we take a closer look at city planning as an element of urban governance, concluding with a brief comment on the question of good governance.

INFORMAL URBAN GOVERNANCE

In the view from Beijing, the administrative areas of the empire constituted a nested hierarchy whose lowest level was the rural county, rising through prefecture, circuit, and province to the culminating point in the imperial capital itself. These five levels embraced the entire national territory and constituted a unified administrative field ruled from the center.[5] Each level had a designated city as its administrative capital. Capital cities were distinguished from most other cities by having imposing walls, gates, and towers rising above the gates, symbols of imperial might. Most also featured an orthogonal layout of streets and city gates. Within the city walls stood the walled government compound, the *yamen*, which comprised not only the offices of the local magistrate (or prefect, or governor) but, as a rule, his living quarters as well. The formal powers of his office extended to the limits of the administrative level over which he presided. Although there might be other cities besides the capital within his territory, the vast majority of imperial subjects were engaged in farming. As the administrative capital, the county seat was merely the lowest level in a unified hierarchy of governing centers within the vast landscapes of rural China. Although cities might be important as trading hubs, for their specialized manufactures, or as garrison bases, they had no separate identity as a polity apart from their status in the hierarchy of imperial governance.[6] John Watt (1977) describes the *yamen* of a county-level city during the Qing dynasty:

> Of the many public offices at various levels of the Ch'ing government, the county-level yamen had greatest impact on the lives of the people because it was the most immediate and frequently encountered form of imperial authority. The county yamen served also as the main center for negotiation between bureaucratic government and informal local authority. This *sub rosa* activity was an important function of the county yamen as its most visible public undertaking. In short, the county-level yamen served both as the leading instrument of public authority and as the primary arena of political exchange. Because of the diversity and significance of these functions, the county yamen was an exceptionally busy institution, astir "from sunrise to sunset." (353)

For the central government, he continues, "the county yamen was the principal office for carrying out administrative policies. Within the state apparatus as a whole, the metropolitan administration formulated imperial policies and supervised their execution. The provincial, circuit, and prefectural administration acted as intermediaries between the central government and the county level. But it was up to the roughly 1,500 county-level yamens, and in

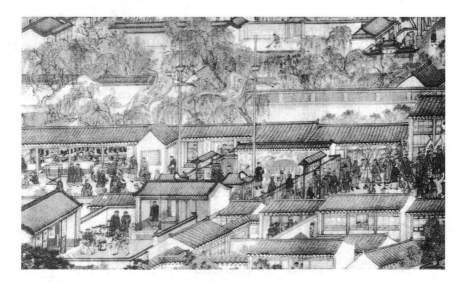

Compound of the provincial government (*yamen*) in Suzhou

particular to their magistrates, to apply these policies to the populace and to see that they were respected" (361).

Implementing imperial policies might not, however, describe precisely what county magistrates were actually expected to do. Their formal responsibilities were principally to maintain public order, oversee the construction of public works (city walls, dikes, bridges, and so on), and collect taxes. Much of their time was taken up with the administration of justice. "For the people at large, the county yamen served as the court of first instance in civil disputes. Despite widespread popular distrust of the yamen because of the rapacity and severity of its personnel, litigation seems to have been a prevalent phenomenon in Ch'ing society and regulations existed requiring officials to hear suits within certain time limits" (ibid., 363–64). As for collecting taxes, that was the task of the despised "runners" who scurried across the countryside to harass peasant households and incidentally also to line their own pockets. Magistrates were ever reluctant to venture forth from the city into the surrounding villages. They much preferred to do business with local notables who crowded into their offices "from sunrise to sunset." And because their local tour of duty was usually less than three years—magistrates were frequently rotated to ensure that they would not be co-opted by local gentry—they were under a good deal of pressure to make as much money in a short time as they could. In fact, says Watt, "the county yamen could well be characterized as in business to sell administration at the highest marketable rates" (364).

In a grassroots perspective, the view of what constituted good governance was, not surprisingly, very different. Because of the exorbitant tax extractions and periodic demands for forced labor, in return for which there were few perceived benefits, the yamen was widely detested and among the first institutions to be disbanded after the proclamation of the republic. As far as the local gentry and other members of the elite were concerned, they had to deal with the imperial delegates, but matters of urban governance were left largely to their own discretion.

Qing urban society was densely patterned with networks of local associational life. Temples celebrating local saints (deities) were the focus of neighborhood life, and neighborhood associations took responsibility not only for the ritual purity of the area but also for its general order, harmony, and cleanliness. According to Skinner, citing the work of C. K. Yang, "normal collective operations of urban life such as fire prevention, garbage removal, . . . maintenance of . . . order in the street neighborhood, certain types of . . . charity and religious celebrations, were all traditional parts of neighborhood associations, which were self-governing bodies" (Skinner 1977d, 547). Yang had focused his researches on Foshan in Guangdong Province. But in the interior city of Chongqing, where a federation of merchant associations "operated an orphanage, an old people's home, and a granary, and organized disaster relief and charitable work among the poor," as well as maintaining fire-fighting brigades, the role of local civil society was much the same (550). For the final years of the Qing dynasty, Ma Min provides a similar and quite detailed picture for Suzhou (Min 2002).

But could charitable works like this be called a form of urban self-government, or was it something else altogether? Granted that essential public tasks were being performed, but, to paraphrase Gertrude Stein, in a city of sojourners and immigrants, "there was no self there," no symbolic focal point around which the population as a whole could rally.[7] In the absence of a civic government, there were also no expectations about appropriate standards of urban management. Local magistrates were thus quite willing to allow merchant and temple associations to perform such good works as they were ready to undertake, but this was an informal arrangement for which no one was held accountable. At any rate, imperial funds were generally unavailable for such purposes. Informal city administration of this sort would continue right on through the period of the republic, even in the former imperial capital of Beijing, once the nationalist government of the Guomindang had abandoned that city in favor of Nanjing (Strand 1989).

AN AVATAR OF CITY GOVERNMENT

The dissolution of the ubiquitous *yamen* called for its replacement as the local center of official authority. Ad hoc municipal offices were established in Beijing and Canton (Guangzhou) as early as 1914, and the practice soon spread to other cities. Not until 1921, however, did Canton formally establish a city hall under Sun Yat-sen's younger son, Mayor Sun Fo (Tsin 2000, 23–25). The municipal offices of Beijing were not formally set up until 1928, when the recently relocated central government in Nanjing appointed a mayor to oversee the operation of eight bureaus, including public security, social affairs, public works, public health, finance, education, public utilities, and land (Strand 1989, 224). But it was the police (public security) that absorbed the lion's share of the budget.

In the popular mind, the newfangled policemen had merely replaced the *yamen* runners, but the facts were more complicated than that. As early as

1902 a modern police force had been set up as part of the Qing New Policies program. Trained by the Japanese (who in turn had learned from German models) and outfitted with modern uniforms, police survived the transition to the republican era and, at least in Beijing, were soon to make a name for themselves. It may be worth quoting David Strand's (1989) account at some length.

> By the teens and twenties Beijing had earned the distinction of being "one of the best-policed cities in the world." This reputation was based not on arrest records or skill at crime detection but on the "semipaternal way" in which police would "look after the city, settling little disputes that arise over collisions on the street, giving advice here and there." In addition to mediating disputes, controlling traffic, and fighting crime, the police also regulated all manner of economic, cultural, and political activities. The imperial gendarmerie had also taken order-keeping to include a range of tasks beyond the narrower mandate of crime prevention. In displacing the gendarmerie, the Beijing police seemed to have absorbed their predecessor's taste for a broad-gauged approach to the maintenance of order. Policemen enforced hygiene standards in the food business, made sure that public toilets were cleaned regularly, gave licensing exams to medical practitioners, regulated the storage in temples of coffins awaiting shipment back to the deceased's hometown or village, and tried to prevent the indiscriminate dumping of toxic or contaminated waste. Policemen censored public entertainments and political expression. They supervised a variety of institutions designed to administer to and control the city's poorest residents, including soup kitchens, schools, reform schools, and workhouses. After close study, the premier Western student of Beijing society during the Republican period, Sidney Gamble, concluded that the police were "responsible for most of the [governmental] work done in the city and touch almost every side of the life of the people." (71–72)

In Strand's felicitous expression, the police were the "avatar of government," the visible agents of a civic order in the new dispensation. Turmoil and chaos might reign beyond the city walls, but in the city itself the appearance of calm and order had to be maintained. A photograph of Beijing taken on a clear summer day in the early 1920s shows a placid flow of rickshaws and pedestrians moving leisurely toward two city gates. A street-widening project is in progress. The divided roadway, lined with broad sidewalks, is clean. Placed at regular intervals for as far as the eye can see, at least seven uniformed policemen are visible, maintaining public order.[8]

The police were the agents of a visible order, but on whose behalf did they act? In a period when the national state was weak and civil society resilient, the time-honored ways of informal governance encouraged the idea of shared responsibilities. There were many new actors on the scene, but the merchant elites continued to play their role. "While the police sought to administer the city," writes Strand (1989), "organizations representing merchants, lawyers, bankers, students, workers, and other groups attempted to police their own ranks and influence the behavior of other groups, including the police. In this politically complex, pluralistic process, the Beijing chamber of commerce played a critical role in handling a range of issues related to public order, from welfare policy to city planning" (98–99).

AN URBAN PLANNING MANIFESTO

We have already met Sun Fo as Guangzhou's first mayor. Sun had been sent abroad by his father to study at the University of California and Columbia University. Returning in 1916, he soon turned to civic matters and became an ardent champion of modern city planning. In an essay published in 1919 he argued for the virtues of a scientific approach to planning that would lay out the city's future as an exemplary model.

> Sun Fo pronounced that "investigation" and "survey" constitute essential tools for urban planning. The scope of investigation, he wrote, should cover every aspect of society and the economy. It must contain all the facts that can be put in statistical form. To construct an urban center, investigation should be made of the population in the area, the different occupations of the residents, the nature and quantity of local products, and the amount and variety of present and future trade. In addition, surveys must be conducted. . . . It is clear that Sun Fo saw critical linkages in these different sets of data. Again, the emphasis is on producing accurate statistics, which in turn requires a well-equipped official organization as well as detailed thorough investigation. (Tsin 2000, 23)

Here was a manifesto for a new technocratic order. At the beginning of the 1920s, urban planning, according to Sun, had three major objectives: to prepare a city for the communication needs of the future, to improve its sanitation needs, and to provide open spaces for recreational use, particularly urban parks. Its ultimate aim, however, was more ambitious: "to transform the conditions in which people ordered their everyday lives by reaching into the realms of their daily practices, right down to the level of hygiene and patterns of entertainment" (24). Scientific planning would force people to become modern.

MAOISM: THE WORK-UNIT CONCEPT OF THE CITY

Sun Fo's ideas did not have enough time to become fully operative, even though during the 1920s and 1930s the Chinese city underwent enormous physical changes in a desperate attempt to overcome centuries of stagnation.[9] Despite warlordism, Japanese invasion, and civil war, city-building went on apace. In 1949, however, all this came to a halt with the ascension to power of the Chinese Communist Party (CCP). While the CCP sought to consolidate a half-century of city-building during its first decade of rule, Mao's more radical vision took over from 1958 onward. Rural society would be restructured around the collective work of communes while the new urban order would be based on the socio-spatial concept of the work unit or *danwei*. Spatially, the *danwei* was a walled compound organized around a state-owned enterprise or other institution (educational, research, or administrative). Its work force was housed in what was to be a minuscule version of a full-fledged socialist society. Small apartments were to be provided at nominal prices. Collective provision would be made for basic health care and child care, as well as educational and recreational services. From cradle to grave, people would have little reason ever to leave the walled domain of the *danwei*. For retired workers, the "iron rice bowl" would ensure a dignified old age and an appropriate funeral in the end (Perry and Lü 1997). The pluralist, "anarchic" city of the republican era, together with its informal governance system, would be restructured into something that resembled Tang dynasty Chang'an, flavored with a strong dose of a Legalist doctrine of pre-Han origin.

This project was never completely carried out, and much of the "disorderly" old city remained standing. But urban planners were not required for its implementation. New *danwei* had to be sited, of course, but beyond productive infrastructure, much of which was directly linked to work units, urban investments were held to an absolute minimum. The "bourgeois" city of consumption had to be transformed into the socialist city of production. By 1960 physical planning had become all but superfluous, and during the Cultural Revolution its practice was completely suspended. With few exceptions, mainly involving the construction of new industrial cities in the interior and the reconstruction of Tangshan after a destructive earthquake had leveled the city, physical planning would not be resumed for another generation (Yeh and Wu 1998, 177–78).

RESTORATION OF THE REPUBLICAN-ERA MUNICIPAL SYSTEM

With the consolidation of the reform-era regime in the 1980s, important changes occurred in the governance of cities (Wu 2002; Zhang 2002b). The work-unit system continued, but *danwei* were no longer required to provide housing and basic social services, which would now become a municipal function. An effective municipal government was resurrected in the image of the republican-era municipal office, though with significant differences. In the redefinition of municipality in 1984, nearby counties and county-level cities were placed under its jurisdiction, so that, in addition to its own urban districts, a central municipality would also be responsible for the management of surrounding rural areas (where collective land ownership prevailed) and county-level cities (where land was held by the state). Thus, city and countryside were once again merged into a single administrative unit, as they had been under the Qing. Within this framework, however, rural counties might at any time be "annexed" to the metropolitan center by raising their status to that of urban district.

Industrial work unit (*danwei*) housing and factory in Beijing, 1992. This area has since been redeveloped as community housing.

Municipality and urban district are now distinct levels of government in that both are supposed to respond to legislative assemblies—the local People's Congresses—that are enabled to pass laws and make regulations (by-laws). These assemblies are beginning to assert their right to instruct the local administration.[10] In a deeper sense, of course, neither district nor municipality is self-governing. Both must conform to the dictates of the Communist Party, while their actions are constrained by both national legislation and State Council policies. Still, Chinese cities have recovered a good deal of their prerevolutionary autonomy. Among other powers conferred on the municipality, it is required under the City Planning Act of 1989 to prepare comprehensive urban plans, issue land use and building permits, and enforce development controls.

To complete this skeletal account of local governance structure, we must consider two additional levels: Street Offices and Residents' Committees. Both are carry-overs from the Maoist era when they played complementary roles to the dominant work-unit system. At present, however, their role, particularly that of the Street Office, has assumed central importance. As a subdistrict unit, Street Offices (SOs) operate at the interface between "society" and government. They could even be called an "intermediate" institution in Philip Huang's "third realm" (see chapter 5). Here is how Tingwei Zhang (2002b) describes the functions of a typical Street Office in Shanghai:

> In recent years, with the success of the "separating government administration from enterprise operation" policy in production, a new policy of "separate government function from society function" has been initiated. With the withdrawal of municipal government, district governments and SOs are expected to play a more active role in community life. There is a "division of responsibility" between districts and SOs: district governments focus on economic development issues, SOs are expected to manage service for communities. In Shanghai, the SOs official functions have increased from three to eight, and the areas in which SOs are involved have increased from 3 to 15. . . . The SOs new responsibilities include local justice, community security, traffic control, fire protection, sanitation, streetscaping, maintenance of open spaces, environmental protection, family planning, employment and labor force administration, day care service, disaster protection, collective-owned businesses, community services, and farmers' markets. These changes demonstrate a shift of the SO from a low-level administrative body obeying higher government's decisions to a more independent entity representing local interests. (312–13)

Zhang doesn't tell us how well any of these services are actually performed. Moreover, his account is limited to Shanghai, where the average Street Office has a population of 100,000 and covers an area of about 10 km². The stories of other cities may well be different.

Residents' Committees differ from Street Offices in that they are, in the rhetoric of the revolutionary period, a "self-organized mass organization." Under Mao, Residents' Committees were supposed to be elected and play their role under the guidance of a "base-level" government or one of its sending agencies. "In reality," writes Fulong Wu (2002), "the Residents' Committees . . . were financed by local government under the budget for administrative expenditure. Residents' Committees undertake many tasks assigned by the government, such as the maintenance of public order, basic welfare provision and mobilising people during political movements. Typically, a Residents' Committee is in charge of 100–600 households and is staffed by 7 to 17 people" (1084). As Zhang (2002b) observes, while membership in Residents' Committees (at least in Shanghai) is chiefly on a voluntary basis, many committees are actually headed by paid district government employees (313). It would seem that upper-level tiers are still trying to manage life at the grass-roots, even though the relationship is intended to be one of mutuality rather than strictly top-down control. Moreover, new organizations, such as Property Owners' Associations and Business Owners' Associations, are beginning to appear as more effective champions of local interests than the somewhat moribund Residents' Committees of the old era (317–19).[11]

In urban administration the old favorite model of Chinese boxes within boxes is thus alive and well. It seems a logical enough system, so long as the intention is to control the daily behavior of urban residents and to maintain an outward appearance of orderly calm, or what David Strand calls "stateliness." But the control functions of public administration seem to have given way to a new entrepreneurialism, and here the static notion of "boxes within boxes" is no longer good enough.

THE ENTREPRENEURIAL CITY

Since the reforms, cities have had to learn to become entrepreneurial. Throughout the 1980s and 1990s, they had to absorb all sorts of new functions, even as the central government was no longer disposed to share its revenues with municipalities. As mentioned above, financing municipal development had to come from two principal sources: the sale of land use rights and the income from collectively owned businesses. I turn now to the first of these.

Urban land reform was written into the Constitution of 1982, as amended in 1988, and spelled out in greater detail in a series of State Council regulations. All urban land was declared to be the property of the state, while all rural land was the collective property of (administrative) villages. But the right to use a given parcel of land can be transferred (by the local state) to *danwei* for their own use and/or leased to developers on a long-term basis, usually for seventy-five years. As part of their lease agreement, real estate development companies that acquire the right to build are required to clear the site, level the land, and put in the appropriate infrastructure in support of their project (Wong and Zhao 1999, 115).[12]

Hong Kong geographers Wong and Zhao (1999) distinguish between the "formal" process of land transfer, which begins with an application by a prospective land user and requires three levels of approval, and the "informal" process, which is what happens in a majority of cases.[13] Though not illegal in itself, the informal process provides many opportunities for "side payments," which the authors, in an ironic aside, refer to as *guanxi* fees (117–19). The main features of the informal process can be represented as follows. The ball starts rolling when the municipality sets up parcels of land for sale and "looks for reliable agents."[14] In a footnote, however, we are informed that a "reliable agent" is anyone fortunate enough to have access to the decision-making authorities on land apportionment, and is often a close relative or associate of influential government officials (118 n.8). On behalf of the land administration bureau, these agents proceed to conduct informal negotiations with prospective developers, facilitate government approval, and help to "balance the interest of local authorities and developers." Money changes hands. As China's new cities—apartments, office towers, and high-rise luxury hotels— soar skyward, developers, investors, and speculators buy up land use rights (LURs) from the local state, trade LURs in the secondary market, and/or initiate construction on their own.

What is notable in this account is that actual transactions overflow the neat boundaries of the set of Chinese boxes that is supposed to guarantee an orderly city but actually leads to the endemic corruption of the system. There are many hair-raising stories that, on occasion, even make it into the Chinese-language press. Here is one from the *Far Eastern Economic Review* (2003a):

> With workers outside his door preparing to finish razing his neighbourhood, Yu
> Suzhen, a wiry 43-year-old, paces angrily as he describes his fight against tycoon
> Chau Ching-ngai, or Zhou Zhengyi as he is known in his native Shanghai. Yu's

eyes frequently bulge in anger as he and a dozen neighbours tell the *Review* how Chau plans to clear their homes in the centre of Shanghai and build a luxury development.

They're sitting in a house that's still standing—though the electricity, gas, and water lines were cut off for four days in May. Outside the area looks like a war zone. Its residents have protested quietly in recent weeks. Some days earlier, He Shengqin, an older man, put on his army uniform and medals and posed for a photograph in front of his soon-to-be-demolished home. In broad brush strokes, he wrote on a sign the part of the Chinese constitution that protects individual rights.

In many ways, they are the other side of the glitzy real-estate development game where Chau made his wealth. Yu sputters about the helplessness of Shanghai's *laobaixing*—the city's common people—as he flips angrily through papers filed in the lawsuit that his neighbours have brought against Chau.

These papers say that Chau's development firm, Jiayun Investment, received usage rights for a large site along Beijing Road in the middle of Shanghai effectively for free—with usage payment of only 1 renmimbi (12 U.S. cents) per square meter per year. Jiayun holds 99 percent of the rights for the prime piece of land, a block off Nanjing Road where the city's most expensive offices are situated. The other 1 percent is held by a development company owned by the Jingan district government.

The favourable nature of the deal means that Chau should have given the local residents the right to flats in the new development. But nobody told them. Instead, they were offered sums that were not nearly enough to buy a new home in Shanghai. "They never told us that we had the right to move back," Yu shouts, his neighbours nodding in agreement. One man says he got the amount bumped up from 132,440 renminbi to 320,000, but only by paying a 20,000-renminbi bribe to a go-between with the district government.

The man who told them they have a right to stay was Zheng Enchong, a 53-year-old Christian who has advised thousands of Shanghainese in legal disputes with local government and developers. But on June 9, *Shanghai Liberation Daily* said that Zheng had been arrested for "illegally obtaining state secrets," a charge that can cover any information related to government that's not specifically cleared for release.

Zheng told the *Review* just before he was detained that he was used to police pressure and hoped to draw attention to graft, or, as he put it, the "black curtain" in Shanghai real-estate. He said he was inspired by Jiang Yanyong, a retired Beijing doctor who blew the whistle on the cover-up about Severe Acute

Respiratory Syndrome. But Zheng may not be as lucky as Jiang. Officials already confiscated Zheng's license to practise law and the party now looks set to stifle his voice.

Zhou Zhengyi was arrested in 2003, but on a different charge of major bank fraud, which is a national crime. For its part, the Shanghai government seems intent on quashing popular protests over the outcome of an "informal" land clearance project that, even though it is not illegal, nevertheless masks what must have been an enormous amount of graft by municipal officials who had leased land use rights at 12 cents per square meter when the developer—one of China's richest men—can expect to realize a potential gain of more than $600 per square meter.[15] The national government fitfully tries to clamp down on especially execrable levels of corruption, but these well-publicized affairs are only the tip of the iceberg.[16]

WHEN THE BUSINESS OF GOVERNMENT IS BUSINESS . . .

The heady mix of fragmented markets, profiteering, administrative land transfers, speculation, endemic corruption, increasingly desperate attempts to uphold the pyramid-like system of central control over local affairs, gung-ho capitalism, ancient poverty, and crass new wealth give the appearance less of the calm stateliness of 1920s Beijing (as in that old photo) than of a frenzied construction site. Much of this apparent lack of coherence—the sheer, exuberant chaos of it—is the result of (and is reflected in) the dual nature of municipal governance, which is part stately bureaucracy, part buccaneer capitalism. X. L. Ding (1994) has a name for it. He calls it an "amphibious institution." "The notion of 'institutional amphibiousness' highlights indeterminacy in the character and functions of individual institutions, and of boundaries among them. It also highlights the interweaving and interpenetration of different forces at play in political transitions" (299). Ding subsequently broadens his argument to characterize East Asian states more generally, not merely contemporary China. "In East Asia, the states are organizationally pervasive, without clear-cut boundaries. Their powers and functions are diffuse, and they pay little respect to due process. Consequently, the lines between public and private, political and personal, formal and informal, official and nonofficial, government and market, legal and customary, and between procedural and substantial, are all blurred" (317). This blurring of boundaries—despite advances in mathematics (fuzzy sets, fractal geometry) and postmodern rejection of all dualisms—is to a rationalist mind perhaps the most

New high-rise office development in inner-city neighborhood, Shanghai, 1999

puzzling and ultimately troublesome aspect of local governance in China. But if amphibiousness is an enduring characteristic of East Asian states (and perhaps of all indigenous institutions), what is now so often described as merely a transitory phenomenon—as though China were in some sort of inevitable "transition" to . . . what? a globalized market economy with a veneer of democratic institutions?—may well turn out to be a permanent feature of the country's political landscape. Form and substance in this landscape no longer coincide, as urban developments leap across boundaries and conceptual niceties. Interminable, face-to-face negotiations, or *guanxi,* are part of this pattern. We already saw some evidence for this in the informal practices of urban governance in the late Qing dynasty where their physical sites were the *yamen*, guild hall, and neighborhood temple. The amphibious nature of present-day institutions in their boundary-spanning practices is but another instance of the same phenomenon.[17]

Fulong Wu speaks of the entrepreneurial endeavors of reform-era government (Wu 2002). He links the behavior of municipal government to the neo-liberal practices of globalizing city governments, such as the privatization of urban services, user charges on infrastructure, converting managerial departments into profit-seeking companies, and so forth (1085). But a much more telling example of amphibiousness is his account of Street Office business activities in Shanghai:

> Street Offices began to set up small stores and shops, and then gradually to develop these ventures into a wide range of commercial and industrial businesses. Some Street Offices even developed joint ventures with foreign investors to take advantage of location and land. Since the 1990s, then, Street business has become the second-largest local fiscal income generator. The new resources allow Street Office managers to expand their social functions and services such as assistance to poor groups. Street Office managers also benefit from the increasing extra-budgetary income and become an "admired professional group." (1086)

What is interesting about this brief account is the clearly amphibious character of the Street Office. Just as with rural townships and villages, its profit-making businesses are collectively owned. And Street Office social responsibilities can now be fulfilled only because part of the realized profits are recycled into welfare provisions for the poor and into the many other responsibilities with which they are charged. For their good work, Street Office managers are acclaimed as "local heroes." And if they pay themselves what could be interpreted as a "management fee," few local residents are likely to object.

> The opportunity to earn higher salaries provides a direct incentive for the changing behaviour of officials [writes Wu]. Together with the lack of clear regulations on the limits of officials in economic activities [as is typical of amphibious institutions], this creates the space for entrepreneurialism. At the local level, the line between the government and business becomes more blurred than it is in the municipal government. . . . The close relationship between the governing and the governed . . .at the local level forms the basis for entrepreneurial endeavour. (Ibid.)

PLANNING CITIES' FUTURES

For Sun Fo, as we saw earlier, modern planning was less a way to control land uses than a tool for first imagining and then building a new kind of city that could hold its own in comparison with Western and particularly German cities that he so much admired. Sun's project would remain imperfectly and only partially realized for another seventy years. But the processes by which his vision is now carried forward are not perhaps quite what he had imagined.

After two decades when planning was virtually absent from city-building under Maoism, it was officially rehabilitated (and reconstituted) with the City Planning Act of 1989, which set up a comprehensive urban planning system by law for the first time in China.[18] Over the next fifteen years planning expertise was sought chiefly for the production of master plans, which the act had legislated. A closer look at how planning works in practice will give us further insights into the ways of municipal governance in today's China.

In the early years of the new millennium, urban planning is on the way to becoming an important profession. An estimated sixty thousand planners are active at all levels of government, a majority of whom are employed in a handful of large coastal cities. Nationally, planners have formed two associations, one (the City Planners Association of China) with professional, the other (the Urban Planning Society of China) with more academic leanings, and national journals carry on a lively professional discourse. Not all the planners are fully trained in that profession. Those working in municipal planning bureaus, for example, are government officials whose principal role is to ensure that regulations are followed. Professionally trained planners generally work in planning institutes that have responsibility for master planning, design work, and research, while a few have set up private consulting practices

(Zhang 2002a). These institutes are "amphibious" organizations *par excellence*. Nominally under the supervision of the planning bureau, with an off-budget income, they have a good deal of operational autonomy in practice.[19]

Much of what planners do can be summed up as preparing urban master plans (or Comprehensive City Plans, as they are called) that are supposed to guide everyday decision-making on land use, facility location, and transport, and so to help shape city form. All cities are required to have master plans, a tradition that goes back to the 1950s, when many Chinese planners were sent to the Soviet Union to study. Xu and Ng (1998, table 1) have analyzed fifteen such plans for the city of Guangzhou between 1954 and 1993; eleven of them were drawn up in the eight years before city planning was put on ice in the 1960s and planners were sent down to the countryside to be reeducated. Their study is interesting as regards the assumptions used concerning time horizons, population projections, and goals and objectives. At the start of this veritable avalanche of plans in 1954, no fewer than four were prepared for periods varying from fifteen to fifty years. Initially, assumptions about future population were set at 2.2 million, but the last plan in the series (1962) had reduced this to 1.6 million, reflecting the government's intentions to de-urbanize China's cities. Significantly, all four plans were meant to transform Guangzhou from a "city of consumption" into a "city of production." Rapid industrialization through heavy industry, in typical Soviet style, was the order of the day.

Nineteen fifty-five yielded a harvest of three master plans. Their major objective was the Marxist dream to "reduce the differences between town and country." Urban population would be cut back still further, to 1.45 million, with time horizons now more reasonably set at fifteen to twenty years. Plans continued to be drawn up in 1956 and 1957, geared to "facilitate socialist development and industrialization"; the last two plans in 1959 and 1962, before planning was shut down altogether, were ostensibly made to "develop the city of Guangzhou into an industrial base for southern China." This time around, future population estimates were pushed up again to between 1.85 and 2.5 million, and the time frame was set at ten to fifteen years.

When planning fitfully resumed in 1972 and again in 1977, the new goal became "creating a socialist production city and a foreign trade centre." Except for the new reference to a "foreign trade centre," this was the tired old language of Maoism. It wasn't until 1984, and again in 1993, with the reformist era already in full swing, that objectives broke significantly with earlier rhetoric. Over the next twenty to twenty-five years, planning was to "provide adequate public facilities, improve the living environment, and promote a sustainable development" of the city, with its population pegged at 2.8 million.[20]

As is evident from this brief account, master planning during the Maoist period was a formal exercise that followed the party line and had little to do with actually "shaping" urban development. The main practical task left to planners was finding appropriate sites for new *danwei* enterprises. In the most recent set of plans, however, one begins to sense concerns that are more often questions than doctrinal assertions. In 1993, for example, self-identified planning tasks were set out as follows:

> To determine rationally city development goals for the coming century
>
> To examine how socialist market reforms have affected city planning and development mechanisms with reference to the floating population, economic restructuring, provision of infrastructure and hub-center development, and so forth
>
> To emphasize plan implementation
>
> To emphasize the planning of transportation (e.g., highway) networks and the ecology of the cityscape
>
> To combine development and control, and to integrate long-term with short-term planning (Xu and Ng 1998, 44–45)

An agenda such as this indicates an increased professionalism on the part of planners, as well as a greater sense of local autonomy in the context of the Chinese party-state. But to this observer, it seems more like an agenda for research than for action.

The challenges facing today's planners are enormous. There is a new scale to planning. Large cities now "lead" several counties, so planners must consider the city-region as a whole. Migration has swelled population and is clearly putting enormous pressure on public facilities and provisioning. Coordination must be effected with various government departments, especially the Land Management Bureau. In the semi–market economy of China today, urban development proceeds at breakneck speed and must somehow be coordinated with long-range planning for infrastructure, housing, open spaces for recreational use, and so forth. New demands have been put on planning with the challenge of improving the quality of the environment and building "livable" cities. Plan implementation has become an urgent requirement, even as the number of actors who are potential stakeholders in city growth has multiplied; the list now includes not only government bureaucrats across a range of departments and districts, but also foreign investors, local development companies, the People's Congress at city and district levels, property and business owners' associations (that is, the new, increasingly vocal middle class), powerful *danwei*, and others.

There are calls, chiefly from scholars mindful of international practice, for a more participatory approach to planning that goes beyond the interests of powerful stakeholders and their personal *guanxi* relations with gatekeepers in the government. Mee Kam Ng, a University of Hong Kong professor of planning, is one of them. She laments the lack of a participatory culture in both her native city and the mainland showcase city of Shenzhen, immediately to the north of the SAR (Ng 2002). Still, she notes that there are various channels of communication, especially via the mass media, between people and the government. She also observes that the recent establishment in Shenzhen of an Urban Planning Board composed of both official and unofficial members "has helped to improve the legitimacy of land use planning and cultivate a general respect for the legal status of land use plans" (21). But Ng's vision for participatory planning seeks the inclusion in the planning process of ordinary people, of people without a public voice. And this, of course, is not what is happening, either in Shenzhen or, to any significant extent, in Hong Kong.[21]

Anthony Yeh and Fulong Wu, in one of the best informed and most thoughtful discussions of the evolving system of physical planning in China's cities, conclude with a series of recommendations. Their critique is summarized as follows:

> The present planning system should be streamlined and the utopian vision of "comprehensive control" should be abandoned. Efforts should be directed to the strengthening of the statutory status of urban planning; the setting up of the urban planning commission within the local people's congress; and the designation of the urban districts through statutory procedures so as to put all land in the urban fringe under planning control. An independent planning appeal system should be set up to handle disagreements in planning decisions and to reduce administrative discretion of the planning authority. Better coordination between the planning authority and the land authority is needed and more public participation should be introduced. The role of planners in society and land development should be rethought. Professionalism in urban planning should be formed with the establishment of a professional planning institute to monitor and improve the professional standards and planning education of planners. (Yeh and Wu 1998, 247)

The merits of these suggestions for a better institutional setup for planning will no doubt continue to be debated. Urban governance in China is in a state of constant experimentation and flux. It has to respond to an enormous variety of local conditions. The situation is immediately apparent as soon as one begins to read accounts of planning in, say, the industrial powerhouse of Shenzhen and a very different sort of city, provincial Quanzhou in Fujian Province, which, after Xian and Beijing, is China's third most important historical city.[22] Experiments are everywhere under way. Given the hundreds of cities throughout its immense territory, no single account is likely to give more than a very general idea of how any specific city is actually managed. This chapter is no exception.

I began with the observation that all discussions of governance, including that of city-building, will necessarily have to confront the normative question of what constitutes "good governance." But they must do so in critical awareness not only of traditional answers to the question but also of present realities. From the succession of meanings we have explored in this book—spatial, economic, sociocultural, and political—it will have become apparent that the mixture of improvisation, experimentation, and pragmatic decision-making superimposed upon a rigid system of what I have called Chinese boxes is, for all of its ingenuity, an inadequate response. The system remains, in the language of François Jullien, "opaque."[23] The emperor is in hiding, but life in the empire doesn't run like clockwork, as the Legalists of old had imagined that it would once the emperor was rendered invisible. Ding introduced the concept of amphibiousness to account for a state that frantically tries to cope with the impossible. But the walls of the boxes are beginning to crack, and the once homely *guanxi* relations have given birth to monsters like Chau Ching-ngai awaiting the outcome of the government's criminal investigations into his financial house of cards.

The primitive capitalism that characterizes the present era operates under a smokescreen that protects the system from criticism by its subjects. But little by little, a system such as this loses legitimacy, until one day popular criticism erupts in massive protest. On July 3, 2003, half a million people demonstrated in Hong Kong to express their dissatisfaction with the process of formulating the national security legislation under Article 23 of the Basic Law governing the SAR. In an e-mail I received the following day, my informant writes: "I think the march showed that Hong Kong has entered a new era—and the people's voice is loud and clear—we want a more democratic system, a more accountable government, and a more transparent process.

The gap between the government's stance and the cry of the general public is exceedingly huge!" More democracy, more accountability, more transparency: these are watchwords that might well not only inform the SAR government in how it conducts its business under the formula of "one country, two systems," but also guide a process of thorough-going reform of China's creaky and antiquated system of governance, particularly at the local level.

Conclusion: Backward into the Future

The story I have tried to tell in the preceding chapters is ongoing. This final section of the book is therefore more a kind of stock-taking than a conclusion. What can we learn from the past that might help us understand what is happening in China today? I have touched on a variety of topics that pertain to certain facets of urbanization: new patterns of mobility, rural industrialization, everyday life, urban governance. Many other possible topics have been left out. Of these, perhaps the most important is "sustainability"—that is, the durability and robustness of China's urban transition in ecological, sociocultural, and economic terms. The present pace of transformation has put the country under enormous stress. In the last section of this conclusion, I will identify the nature and severity of these challenges. As a planner, this is my forward perspective: to identify and deal with tasks whose resolution lies ahead. But here the devil is in the detail, and it would take detailed studies of specific cities to come up with new insights rather than merely repeat the comfortable admonitions that the term *sustainability* often gives rise to.

THE DIFFICULT PATH AHEAD

The most challenging task is not to determine the specifics of policy but to move along a *sustainable path of transformation* between the two poles of ever-present danger: the lapse into anarchy and the reimposition of a totalitarian rule leading to stasis. These poles are not imaginary. In the nearly forty years of the republic, anarchy was an ever-present reality in Chinese life, one that surfaced again during the difficult years of the Cultural Revolution. As for totalitarian stasis, it is perhaps best symbolized by the cellular society of the city of *danwei*, the walled work-unit compounds of the urban landscape under Mao Zedong that reached a kind of perfection following the disaster of the Great Leap Forward campaign in the 1960s.

Until well into the reform period, the *danwei* was a self-contained, walled compound that enshrined not only a productive enterprise or service institution such as a hospital or university, but also a "small society" that provided for a complete way of life and personal security into old age. The efficient use of resources was not a major operational criterion of the *danwei*. Labor mobility was minimal, and children who grew up in the compound would typically inherit their parents' jobs on their retirement or be reassigned to other tasks within the unit. Among those who belonged to the *danwei*, there was substantial material equality: they all ate out of the same pot, so to speak, but the world beyond the gate had only a shadowy existence for them. The work-unit concept was meant for urban areas. In the countryside, the commune performed a similar function. Both were intended to be as autarkic as possible, except that the primary function of the commune was to produce surplus grain for urban consumption, while the *danwei* produced, among other things, the basic necessities of life that the peasant commune lacked.

A system so designed, however, was bound to end in stasis, in mere reproduction that stifles creativity. With the reforms beginning in the 1980s, and especially the 1990s, the cellular society was slowly dismantled. The commune system was the first to be abolished. The *danwei* continued but was stripped of many of its social and political functions. Work units now had, above all, to pay attention to market signals; in competitive markets, they had to mind their efficiency. *Danwei* were merged, downsized, or turned into joint enterprises, as their "little societies" gradually gave way to the expanded spheres of personal autonomy described in chapter 5.

Although the stasis of the former regime has been broken, given the diversity of China, the dynamism of its people, the declining faith in the Communist Party as the moral center of society, the unstable mix of the traditional and new, the emergence of new forms of social stratification, and the shattering of old verities, anarchy remains a possibility. In times such as these, people fall back on the institutions and rituals they can trust: kinship, loyal friends, personal connections (*guanxi*). But the center, the CCP, still holds, even though it is no longer the all-knowing, all-powerful center that knows the way and can do no wrong. Power in China is becoming more pluralized. The government is doing what it can, but with far fewer resources than it would need to hold the course. In its wisdom, it has largely decentralized the budget to provincial and, still further, to municipal levels. Although national guidelines are still being issued and are variously interpreted at local levels, they are not strictly enforced and only fitfully adhered to. In order to do what needs doing, local governments become "amphibious," launching themselves into money-making ventures that, when they succeed, are lucrative for both the parties directly involved and the collective interests in whose name business deals are concluded. So long as a rough balance is maintained, everyone is happy; but occasionally, the lucre is beyond what is tolerable, or the gain leads to only personal enrichment with no public benefits, and then the party-state has to step in to rebalance the scales. Given these conditions, what should be done to make the process of transition itself more "sustainable"? Alas, there is no master recipe, and every day is like driving in city traffic, where one has to stay alert, maneuver, take advantage of an opportunity to lurch ahead, stop, then inch forward again. One has to be skilled to do that, and they don't teach those skills in driving school.

What, then, are the lessons of the last twenty-five years of the urban transition? One obvious lesson is that to maintain the precarious balance between stasis and anarchy, continuities are as important as change. The *danwei* system still exists, but its power is greatly diminished now that it has to cope with market forces, domestic competition, and the World Trade Organization. In rural areas the commune system is gone, but the collective at the level of township (the old brigade) and village (the old production team) survives, reinvigorated by profitable ventures of one sort or another, from manufacturing to golf courses. The new forms of economic relations are horizontal, as economic enterprises look to sell in both domestic and overseas markets, but central directives from Beijing cannot simply be ignored, and hierarchy is still a pervasive principle. Even so, local officials can no longer look merely upward to their patrons for guidance; they must also look downward so as to manage things in ways that are more or less acceptable to those over whom they rule. Life has become more difficult. Communist Party organs may, from time to time, still use the hoary expression, "the masses" (as in "the CCP is the vanguard of the masses"), but at ground level local authorities have to deal with a restless version of what, for want of a better term, may be called civil society, with obstreperous peasants, downsized workers, powerful work units, stroppy homeowners' associations, various economic and professional groupings, foreign entrepreneurs, tough-minded women's organizations, desperate pedicab drivers, and on and on, the full panoply of metropolitan actors more or less organized to defend their own interests in rough but fluid times.[1]

It has often been observed that the Chinese are a pragmatic people who don't waste much time on speculative notions but turn their mind to solving the problems set before them. In this, they display diligence, persistence, and a willingness to negotiate differences. Success is measured not by good intentions but by results. It has also been said that the present reformist regime is less ideological than its predecessor, that it displays pragmatic management skills and flexibility, and that it has a realistic assessment of the limits of its still considerable powers. Many of China's present-day leaders were originally trained as engineers, and they tackle their problems with an engineer's mindset. The risks they take are calculated, quite unlike the utopian rashness and political cunning of the Great Helmsman whom they replaced.

And thus, little by little, a new society emerges. What on a stupendous scale is happening in China today is a transformation *from within*. To be sure, there is still central planning, and periodically great rituals are performed that affirm the supremacy of the party-state, but everyday life in villages, neighborhoods, districts, and cities is changing the country in a huge implosion of cultural creativity. Its visible manifestations are the new boulevards and housing estates in the major cities, the sense of empowerment made tangible by the symbolism of the metropolis, its soaring office towers and luxury hotels, its subways, its spectacular bridges, its gigantic construction projects. It would be altogether misleading to discount these achievements, to wish back the nostalgic neighborhoods of Qing dynasty cities, which are being erased or turned into tourist attractions; it would be equally misleading, however, to dwell exclusively on the overwhelming problems that remain.

INTERPRETING THE URBAN TRANSITION

I would like to sum up some of the things we have learned from the experiences of the last twenty-five years. They concern the extent to which urban development has been endogenous; the question of a civil society; the nature of the Chinese city; and the system of urban governance.

An Endogenous Development?

Since the 1980s foreign capital has been pouring into China, much of it coming from Hong Kong (which, of course, is no longer "foreign"), Taiwan (which is officially declared to be a province of China), South Korea, Japan, and the Chinese diaspora, especially from Southeast Asia. There has been a tendency on the part of outside observers to credit this influx of capital for much of the dizzying growth in the coastal provinces of China, including the upsurge of rural industrialization, described in chapter 3. But the *in situ* urbanization we observed is a unique phenomenon replicated, if at all, in only one other country, communist Vietnam. What accounts for this anomaly? There is no simple answer to this question, and any explanation is in some sense overde-termined. I have mentioned the very high population densities in the delta re-gions and the narrow coastal strip in Fujian Province; the old craft traditions in these regions; the entrepreneurial spirit of the local peasantry; the high internal rate of savings; prior experiences with industrial management gained during the harsh years of Maoism; and last, not least, the lingering influence of collective ownership and capable local leadership. I characterized China's rural development as endogenous—that is, as largely self-produced—with for-eign capital playing an important but for the most part complementary role. It is precisely a result of the difficult but necessary process of continuity-in-change in negotiating the middle passage between anarchy and stasis, which, as I have argued, is a hallmark of the Chinese approach to modernization.

A Chinese Civil Society?

China does not, at present, have a civil society in the contemporary Western sense. Its "public sphere" has been absorbed by the party-state, and without it and the democratic institutions that make it possible, a civil society, such as Jürgen Habermas would have it, is inconceivable. China thus presents us with a paradox: an increasingly pluralist society within a monolithic political system. But under the impact of ongoing changes, the system is beginning to open up, with fiscal devolution, increasing economic complexity, greater openness to the outside world, the widespread loss of faith in communist ideology, the growing self-assertion of the National People's Congress and especially its local incarnations, the "amphibiousness" of local institutions, and the strengthening of the legal system in response to the rising number of foreign firms doing business in China, WTO membership, and China's own Legalist inheritance. Urban China currently displays a remarkable capacity for self-organization, reflected in the large number of civil organizations that are nominally under the supervision of the party-state but are beginning to act with a growing sense of autonomy. Given China's statist traditions—a tradition well entrenched throughout East Asia—it is unlikely that a truly autonomous civil society will emerge anytime soon or that it will clamor for an end to authoritarian rule. Not everything depends on the periodic elections of formal democracy, and interest representation can be played out in ways that do not directly challenge the state's supremacy. The concept of a civil society, however, reminds us of the reality of the churning social interests confronting local cadres and individuals in China today. The absence of an independent judiciary, media free to criticize the government, and multiple political parties in the liberal democratic sense does not refute the reality of the plural forces operating in Chinese cities today—what we may call China's actually existing civil society.

The Nature of the Chinese City

As has frequently been noted, the Chinese city, unlike European cities, is not a corporate entity. Yet it is more than merely a *site* where things happen. In chapter 6 I paraphrased Gertrude Stein to the effect that "there is no self there" in the Chinese city. But this may be too rash a judgment. Shanghainese, it is said, are very much aware of living in China's most sophisticated, cosmopolitan city, and are proud of it. And with its still evolving democratic institutions, Hong Kong is displaying a very un-Chinese self-assertiveness, as evidenced by the mass demonstrations in 2003 against the Security Bill promoted by the SAR government at Beijing's bidding, which forced the government to withdraw the proposed legislation. Strong city identities are perhaps still rare in China, and Hong Kong's situation notwithstanding, they have not been translated into anything like self-government. At the same time, however, city administrations are beginning to accept the reality of the millions of temporary worker-migrants in their midst and to make provisions for them in planning urban infrastructure, in a typically pragmatic adjustment. At the same time, central cities have acquired administrative responsibilities over rural counties in their vicinity, which gives their governance a regional character, with country and city melding into each other. While this will tend to diffuse urban identity, it may strengthen self-assertion at the more local levels of township, district, and neighborhood.

Urban Governance

The traditional Chinese system of governance of "boxes within boxes," a forceful assertion of the principle of hierarchy, is beginning to give way under the multiple strains of modernization. The Street Office, a holdover from Maoist times, has acquired extraordinary importance in local city management, and even though it is not an elected body (yet?), in one way or another it has to be responsive to local needs. Yet, at the same time, it needs to make money to fund its public activities and does so by engaging in various business activities, a prime example of institutional "amphibiousness."

Elsewhere, too, cracks are beginning to appear in the hierarchical control system. Some would ascribe this to the perceived high levels of corruption.

But in a country where *guanxi* relations are the way to get things done, where personal relationships based on long-term reciprocities still count for something, it's not always easy to detect outright corruption. Overall, China ranks in the third quintile of all countries worldwide in the perception of corrupt practices. There are, of course, spectacular cases of public larceny that have been exposed and punished. But at least for the time being, the party-state seems able to keep such deviations within limits. Still missing is any system of public accountability of government practices. And scattered attempts to involve the public in land use planning have met with limited success so far. On the other hand, near-universal literacy, a more mobile and savvy society, increasing openness in the media, and growing reliance on legal safeguards all suggest that government will have to pay more attention, not to "the masses" as per old-style communist rhetoric, but to the leading formations of an emerging civil society defending their own interests and making demands regarding what they expect their government to do for them.

THE WAY FORWARD: SUSTAINABLE CITIES?

In setting out the agenda for this small book, I said that the story I am trying to tell, though it has a beginning (and indeed, has a number of possible beginnings), has no proper ending. China's urban transition is an unfinished story. Moreover, its outcome is unpredictable. There are obvious reasons for this, one of which is that what will happen will to some considerable degree be determined by how the Chinese government chooses to tackle the interlocking problems of a sustainable development. As a broad, encompassing goal, sustainability has been widely adopted since the 1992 Earth Summit in Rio de Janeiro, when governments committed themselves to lay out practical strategies on how to meet long-term economic, sociocultural, and environmental objectives, under the common title of Agenda 21. China was the first country worldwide to produce a national Agenda 21 report embracing four principal strategies: a comprehensive strategy and policy of sustainable development; sustainable social development; sustainable economic development; and a strategy of rational resource utilization and environmental protection (Ng, Chan, and Hills 2002). Promoting high rates of economic growth, however, retains its privileged position in the hierarchy of national goals. Since setting forth Agenda 21, the central government has taken many concrete steps to integrate sustainability objectives with overall development, from the national level on down through provincial and prefectural to local levels. But as Ng, Chan, and Hills observe, much remains to be done:

China's response to sustainability issues since the 1992 Earth Summit does appear to reflect a growing realisation that the high rates of economic growth enjoyed by the country over the past two decades will simply not be possible in the future unless it manages processes of environmental and social change more effectively and integrates these with the promotion of economic growth. At the same time, it is also clear that enhancing prospects for sustainable development will depend upon the ability of the central government in Beijing to ensure that its policies and edicts are translated into effective action at the provincial and local levels. It is at these levels that tensions between economic, social and environmental concerns are most acutely felt. Therein, perhaps, rests a key challenge, namely the extent to which a national, top-down strategy for sustainable development can be reconciled with territorial and group interests that are more localised in nature. (18)

In the remaining pages, I shall very briefly sketch some of the sustainability issues for cities that continue to pose major challenges for both local and national policymakers and planners. To do so, I will draw upon existing studies. Two of these concern environmental conditions for large cities: the centrally located metropolis of Wuhan and the southern city of Kunming. A third addresses the rising unemployment problem in Chinese cities. The final study concerns the question of poverty and income inequality in China, with a special focus on urban areas.

The Urban Environment

Wuhan is a large industrial center at the confluence of the Yangzi and Han Rivers, a thousand kilometers upstream from the Yangzi delta. A two-year, British/Chinese study of Wuhan's environmental conditions and policy responses was completed in 1997 (Taylor and Xie 2000).[2] The study has three main conclusions, from which I quote directly.

1. The city's environment is seriously degraded, with an urgent need to treat high concentrations of sulphur dioxide, nitrogen oxides and dust-fall levels. Much of its surface waters are highly polluted, resulting largely from poor treatment of wastewater. In all areas there is an urgent need for improvement. Although the pollution from rural industries will increase in coming years, the main polluters remain the city's state-owned enterprises.
2. Wuhan has a detailed and complex system of laws and regulations

covering most areas, combined with a framework of environmental monitoring and a system of rewards, sanctions and environmental funding.
3. This system is inadequate for meeting the city's current environmental needs . . . dissemination is poor . . . advice given by environmental departments is often ignored [by enterprises] . . . the impact of environmental planning is limited by being implemented at too general a level . . . environmental impact assessment seems to be of poor quality . . . lack of funds . . . lack of clarity in requirements . . . pollution fines are set too low . . . limited funds are available for pollution control. (157)

These conclusions, though specific to Wuhan and now already somewhat dated, may well apply to other large industrial cities in China. They underscore the importance of local measures for a sustainable development. Good environmental monitoring is only a beginning. Enforcement mechanisms exist on paper but are difficult to apply in practice and, when they are applied, may be insufficient to entice state-owned enterprises (SOEs) to alter their behavior, install improved technologies, and cooperate with local government to improve their wastewater treatment. Many Wuhan SOEs have been forced to close their doors because of their inability to survive without government subsidies. Imposing even greater financial burdens on the remaining industries could wipe out dozens more. It is clear, therefore, that insisting on better antipollution measures, important as they are, may have to be balanced against an equally important employment objective. The question of how far to push environmental policies is difficult to answer because of the clear priority the central government has assigned to economic growth, and the general shortage of financial means.[3]

This does not, however, mean that nothing should be done to ameliorate health-threatening environmental conditions. A successful example is reported from the city of Kunming, capital of Yunnan Province (Feiner et al. 2002). With a regional population of 7 million residents plus another million or so temporary workers, Kunming is about the same size as Wuhan. Beginning in the early 1980s the city initiated a cultural exchange program with Zurich, the financial metropolis of Switzerland, which soon expanded into an intensive technical collaboration. Between 1987 and 1994 attention was focused on issues of water supply and wastewater treatment, but already in 1993 this approach was broadened to include transportation as an important component of a sustainable path to development.[4] In 1996 a multicomponent package started to steer the urban dynamics of Kunming toward greater sustainability and to begin implementing the master plan for public transportation that had been drawn up. Over the past nine years, the Netzwerk Stadt und Landschaft (City and Landscape Network) of the Zurich Technical University (ETH) has been deeply involved in conducting workshops and various training activities with Kunming planners. Visible outcomes of this project include the following: (1) an innovative solution for Kunming's bus system in the form of a reserve lane for buses, with two already completed lanes and two more under construction; (2) a short-haul rail system for regional transportation to be put in place by 2005; and (3) the establishment of a historical city preservation office to protect whatever remains of the old city, and the restoration of four model homes. The authors of the Kunming study conclude that "the collaboration with Zurich has demonstrated to Kunming ways to foster urban growth without greater automobile dependence, air pollution and waste of arable land, while maintaining good urban quality. By means of its regional multidisciplinary planning approach, its investments into a strong local and regional pubic transport system, and its efforts to promote environmental protection, Kunming has the opportunity to become a model city for future urban development in China, a model which is most urgently needed" (67). Still, the number of such success stories is quite small.[5] In the two instances known to me, positive results were obtained, in part, because of long-term commitments and close personal relationships between foreign consultants and Chinese officials. Without this, and without adequate funding, technical assistance programs stand very little chance of having significant impacts.

Unemployment and the Threat of Jobless Growth

According to Dorothy Solinger's (2003) deeply researched and pessimistic article "Chinese Urban Jobs and the WTO," 25 percent of China's urban work force, which is estimated at about 200 million, is currently unemployed or only nominally employed.[6] There are several reasons for this excessively large population. I have already mentioned the shutdown or downsizing of many state-owned enterprises in cities like Wuhan. The decline of the overall rate of economic growth since the mid-1990s is another reason. Because of increased competition or mismanagement, rural industries have had to reduce their employment by perhaps a third since the late 1990s. More serious is the rising capital intensity of industrial investments, which means that for every million yuan invested, fewer jobs will be generated. At the beginning of the reform era, job generation was at the historic high of 9 percent per year. This has now sunk to less than 0.9 percent (65n.19). And present demand tends to be for younger workers with a relatively high level of education. Lurking in the near future is the threat of another 100 million agricultural workers whose livelihood will be threatened as World Trade Organization (WTO) rules go into effect. The overall picture, writes Solinger, "is becoming increasingly clear. As China enters even more fully into the global economy, we can expect that, while millions of better placed citizens rise to the challenge and upgrade their jobs, millions more will sink, their working lives cut short, their potential undeveloped, their situation increasingly desperate, and their capacity to purchase any of those enticing products offered up by the world market and its merchants nonexistent" (87). Solinger herself offers no prescriptions. But she worries about the rising waves of protest in cities throughout China, of workers demanding some sort of job security, or the pay-out of pension accumulations to which they are entitled, and other benefits they expect their government to provide. In short, it is no longer just a case of putting economic expansion first and hoping that the jobs will follow. With what is now effectively jobless growth, China's entire modernization project is put in jeopardy. People, and not only in China, expect growth with equity. Failing to get this brings the threat of instability.

Poverty and Income Inequality

In China as a whole, poverty is concentrated in rural areas. Even so, urban poverty has been increasing in recent years, while rural poverty has been declining. Khan and Riskin's estimate (2001) is based on a seven-year statistical study covering the period between 1988 and 1995. Their headcount index of urban poverty is shown to rise steeply over this period, to about 8 percent (77, fig. 4.2), but their sample fails to include layoffs resulting from the downsizing and bankruptcies of state-owned enterprises—which for the most part occurred at a later date—and the large number of temporary migrant workers (the floating population), many of whom would have had to be added to the numbers of the poor.[7]

But poverty in an era of rising expectations is only one side of pervasive and rising income inequality, especially in rural areas. A comparison is instructive. Over the period of their study, the contribution of agriculture to household income fell from 74 percent to 56 percent, while that of wages increased from 9 percent to 22 percent. (This latter estimate reflects the rise of rural industries.) At the same time, the index of inequality (Gini index) increased from 0.34 to 0.43. According to the authors, greater inequality can reasonably be attributed to the growth in the wage component of some households (144).

In towns and cities, income inequality increased even faster, from a low of 0.23 to 0.33 in seven years, a 42 percent gain. Wages grew to 61 percent of household income, retiree incomes rose from 7 percent to 12 percent, and the rental value of owner-occupied housing grew from 4 percent to over 11 percent. According to the authors, housing assets turned out to be a major source of urban inequality. Three-fifths of privately owned housing belonged to the richest 10 percent of the urban population (145; see also Wang 2003). Again, it is important to point out that these figures do not extend to the temporary population in cities, who may constitute as much as one-third of the urban labor force. Had they been included, urban income inequalities would have been substantially greater.

Although the authors undertake separate analyses for urban and rural populations, they see both poverty and income inequality as inextricably linked. Although indicators of urban poverty and income inequality are still relatively low by international standards, the trends are very serious, indeed. A partial solution to this condition would the creation of new jobs, but as we saw, the prospects for this are slim.

The central government appears to be aware of these questions, but its ability to undertake countervailing policies is quite limited. It can instruct, but it cannot always enforce. As Khan and Riskin point out, Beijing's fiscal capacity is one of the lowest in the world (though the government can draw on extra-budgetary resources through the lingering system of a command economy), while local governments increasingly depend on income from their own business activities, including the leasing of public lands for development. There is, moreover, a tradition of urban governance, which, as we saw in chapter 6, leaves much of the detail of local planning to negotiations between local authorities and various business elites. Laissez-faire at that level, constrained only by residual Confucian values, is unlikely to cope effectively with the kinds of sustainability issues I have mentioned. So unless the system of governance is changed *in the direction of greater central direction*, the trends charted here—a degrading environment, rising unemployment, deepening poverty, growing inequality—are likely to continue; they will certainly not disappear of their own accord.[8]

Sustainable cities are not an automatic by-product of the unrestrained operation of market forces. Government intervention is necessary and will require senior levels to step in. Development priorities may need to be rethought. Maximizing economic growth at the expense of everything else will make many existing problems worse. The system of local public finance needs to be revamped, especially with regard to taxing real estate and curbing land speculation. The "amphibiousness" of local institutions should be restrained. Urban transit should be favored over the private automobile. Slowing down the process of commercialization in agriculture, currently under threat by the WTO, would appear to be a matter of high national priority. Undertaking vast afforestation and other conservation projects on degraded lands must be sufficient to halt and, if possible, roll back further desertification. Developing alternative energy sources (solar and wind power) on a large scale will soon become mandatory and may be cheaper than distant pipelines into Central Asia. Private investments in China's interior regions should be encouraged with specific incentives and supported by appropriate infrastructural programs.

This list of countervailing policies could easily be extended. Sustainability requires appropriate actions in both rural and urban areas; the two are inextricably linked. "Steering the middle passage" between anarchy and stasis, which alone can stave off the threatening disaster of the single-minded pursuit of economic growth, is a difficult, delicate set of maneuvers, but the genius of the Chinese people has historically shown itself to be capable of seeking and finding the appropriate balance. One can only hope that the present generation will find the will to do so in the decades ahead. As the ancient *Book of Changes* has it: "Perseverance furthers."

Notes

INTRODUCTION

1. For details, see Gernet 1996; Fairbank 1986.

2. For a detailed explication of these terms, see chapter 3.

3. The anthropologist Aiwah Ong has made a similar and carefully documented argument in her book, *Flexible Citizenship: The Cultural Logics of Transnationality* (1999).

4. For a very readable introduction to these traditions, see Waley (1939) and Graham (1989).

5. See the brilliant study by Abu-Lughod (1989).

1. HISTORICAL TRACES

1. Other regions listed by Wheatley include Mesopotamia, Egypt, the Indus Valley, Mesoamerica, the Central Andes, and the Yoruba territories of southwestern Nigeria. More recent excavations claim to have pushed back the first appearance of walled towns in the mid-Yangzi region, Hubei Province, to as early as 3600 BCE. As for ancient Anyang, no evidence of city walls has been found. Presentation by archaeologist Yan Wenming (Beijing) at the Centre for Chinese Studies, University of British Columbia, September 2003.

2. The traditional dates for Confucius are 551–479 BCE.

3. Wheatley (1971, 450) quotes some lines from the classical Book of Odes that capture the essence of Shang dynasty cities: "The capital of Shang was a city of cosmic order, / The pivot of the four quarters. / Glorious was its renown, / Purifying its divine power, / Manifested in longevity and tranquillity / And the protection of us who come after." In Wheatley's interpretation, this ode exhibits the chief modes of traditional urban symbolism: "the imitation of a supramundane archetype, the symbolism of the center and cardinal orientation, the role of the *omphalos* as a point of ontological transition where supernatural power enters the world, and the parallelism of the macrocosmos and microcosmos. In other words, the imperial capital functioned as an *axis mundi* about which the kingdom revolved, and was laid out as an *imago mundi* in order to ensure the protection and prosperity 'of us who come after.'"

4. The story of the construction of Chang'an is told by Wright (1978, 84–88).

5. A useful complement to Heng Chye Kiang's study of the urban transition from the Sui-Tang to the Northern Song is Yinong Xu's detailed monograph on Suzhou's urban form from its historical beginnings to the end of the imperial era (Xu 2000). See also Steinhardt 1990.

6. According to Timothy Brook (personal communication), walls only became ubiquitous markers of county seats south of the North China Plain in the latter half of the sixteenth century. Walls are expensive, he writes, and take up expensive urban real estate when you build them, so local elites generally lobbied hard against propositions to build them.

7. A fifth tier, the circuit, located between province and prefecture, never achieved full governmental status.

8. For the role of the *yamen,* the administrative hall of a city, as a site of negotiation between imperial representatives and local notables, see Watt 1977.

9. For more detail, see chapter 6.

10. Nonetheless, the city was a distinctive place. In his most recent attempt to clarify the rural/urban contrast, Mote (1999) argues that at least from the late Ming onward, living in cities offered people social freedoms that were unavailable to them in their villages. "The concentration of many people in a limited space produced attitudes that were distinctly urban; city dwellers were accustomed to seeing and interacting with strangers, and the ability to remain a stranger to others among whom one lived gave city dwellers the joys and pains of anonymity" (762). Contemporary Chinese sources, he reports, give the modern reader "images of a life that was rich, comfortable, elegant in the taste of the elite, occasionally vulgar in the ostentation of the very rich, and above all an urban life that was varied and lively almost beyond description." (763).

11. Hankou was one of three cities making up today's Wuhan at the confluence of the Han and Yangzi Rivers. By imperial standards, it was not an administrative seat of the empire, and so was merely a "town," one of the Four Great Towns of the Qing that were singled out because of their preeminent role as commercial centers. See Rowe's study, *Hankow: Commerce and Society in a Chinese City, 1796–1889* (1984).

12. "The final hundred years of Manchu rule appear to have replicated the late Ming in witnessing a growing interest by local elites in responding to practical social problems, an interest that took as its explicit focal point the local community. Behind such activist movement, in both periods, lay a perception of failure in imperial administration" (Rowe 1989, 10).

13. In this connection, it may be useful to recall the physical setting for the emergence of a public sphere in Chinese cities. Yinong Xu has an interesting comment on urban public space in the Chinese city: "Apart from that of the streets, any space of notable size that assumed any unambiguous function in the city most commonly took definite shape in the courtyard. Hence the public urban space. . . . A

purposeful space had to belong, and thus be attached, to a certain social institution physically embodied in a certain building compound. The intramural open spaces without walled compounds consisted of only streets and alleys or vacant land, the latter, apart from constituting part of the area within the city walls, being institutionally not much different from the unoccupied pieces of ground around village houses" (Xu 2000, 199).

In this interpretation, courtyards are the only public space in the city other than streets and alleys. They might be temple courtyards, but also public buildings, such as the Examination Halls or the *yamen* pictured on some scrolls. It was "the courtyard, not individual buildings, that acted as a basic unit of spatial organization of the city ... and ... played an essential role in incorporating all its elements into a coherent whole" (ibid.).

14. As Rowe explains, "the inconceivably ambitious goals of the *pao-chia* [*bao jia*] at Hankow [Hankou], as elsewhere, was the complete regimentation of the population into decimal groups of mutually responsible households, arranged hierarchically under successive levels of headmen. . . . Such regimentation presumed at the minimum an enrolment based on accurate door-to-door surveys of the population, recording each inhabitant by name, family, occupation, and native registry. One goal of this enrolment was in the words of an 1878 Hankow commentator, 'to ferret out those rebellious vagrants who have no local roots'" (1989, 298–99).

15. See also the excellent collection of essays edited by Esherick (1999).

16. The following list is drawn from the excellent study by Chan (1994), especially table 2.1.

17. To complete the picture, by 1990 urban population had risen to 303 million (26.4 percent), and by 2000 to 410 million, or 32 percent (United Nations Centre for Human Settlement 2001, table A1). First results of the census for 2000 are now published, however, and provide a somewhat different set of data, based on a new definition of "urban" that is more in line with international practice. In the census year, China's urban population stood at 459 million (36 percent of total) and is currently growing at 4.7 percent annually. In the decade of the 1990s, close to 60 percent of an increase of 157 million was generated by rural to urban migration, 22 percent by urban reclassification, and 20 percent by urban natural increase (Chan and Hu 2003, table 2, estimation 2, and p. 58).

18. It also severely curtailed inter-city migration.

19. The importance of native place identity in the centuries of imperial China has already been remarked upon. In that perspective, the *hukou* system must have seemed quite natural to many peasant farmers. For more details, see chapter 4.

20. The assertion of power by dynastic governments to move people from one place to another, whether for forced labor, for reasons of collective punishment, for frontier settlement, or for populating empty capital cities, was a practice of long standing that continues in modified form. For example, 1.3 million local residents have been

moved to make way for the rising floods of the Yangzi River behind the imposing barrier of the Three Gorges Dam.

21. Rural industrialization would take off during the first two decades of the reform era (see chapter 3).

22. In the present context, I am using the term *civil society* in its "weak" form, to signify a self-organized associational life. In a heuristic attempt to classify various forms of civil society in this sense, Brook (1997, 25) identifies four categories: locality (village and native place associations); occupation (guilds); fellowship (religious societies, benevolent association, literary clubs); and common cause (policy advocates, political parties). To this list one might wish to add lineage (kinship) associations. For a discussion of theoretical debates about civil society in China, see chapter 5.

2. REGIONAL POLICIES

1. In the developing (capitalist) world, economic disparities among regions generally intensify during periods of rapid economic growth. Some governments have attempted to counter this trend and reestablish some sort of regional equilibrium through so-called growth center policies that involve direct infrastructure development at strategic locations and various kinds of subsidies to capital. These "classical" approaches to regional policy are critically discussed by Friedmann and Weaver (1979).

2. Nevertheless, as Wei reports, "many interior governments have used their increasing administrative powers to protect their resources and markets, by distorting price signals and creating unfair competition to limit market penetration of industrial products produced by other regions. Local protectionism and 'investment hunger' have prompted regions to duplicate projects with little consideration for economies of scale and agglomeration" (Wei 2000, 206). It appears that the traditional regionalism of China is reasserting itself through these efforts, regardless of economic efficiency prescriptions.

3. Regional disparities and, more important, regional poverty were not simply ladder-step phenomena. Disparities just as great can be found even within the belt of coastal provinces (see Wei 2000, 133–139).

4. The volume had its genesis in workshops sponsored by the Academy of the Social Sciences in Australia at the Flinders University in South Australia, Adelaide, and by the Chinese Academy of Science at the Institute of Geography, Beijing.

5. For Shanghai and its hinterland, see Yeung and Sung 1996; Wei 2000; and Marton 2000.

6. Major studies of the Pearl River delta include Vogel 1989; Tracy 1997; Lin 1997; Yeung and Chu 1998; and Yeh et al. 2002.

7. Hong Kong became a special administrative region of the PRC in 1997, and two years later Macao was reincorporated into China on similar terms.

8. Fujian Province, along with Xiamen's designation as a special economic zone, was the other specially favored area, intended to capture investments from Taiwan.

Shanghai was not "liberated" to undertake its own drive for modernization until a decade later.

9. Manufacturing employment in Hong Kong had topped out at 47 percent of total employment in 1971; it declined to 41 percent in 1981 and then plunged to 28 percent in 1991 and still further, to 11 percent, in 1999. "Hong Kong companies," writes Vogel, "moved their manufacturing across the border at a frightening speed. . . . In a number of cases taken to court, Hong Kong workers showed up at work in the morning to find the factory empty, the machinery having been moved across the border during the night" (1989, 445).

10. The Gini ratio is a widely used statistical measure of inequality. A ratio of 0 would mean complete equality in the distribution of, for example, income. In this situation, 10 percent of the population in a given region would receive 10 percent of the income generated, and so on for each percentile. A ratio of 1, on the other hand, would imply a situation of complete inequality. In practice, actual income inequalities calculated on a national or regional basis range from about 0.30 (relatively equal) to 0.65 (very unequal).

3. URBANIZATION OF THE COUNTRYSIDE

1. For changes in the definition of designated cities and towns, see Zhu 1999, appendix 1.

2. Following a stratification mix developed by Thomas Heberer, anthropologist Gregory Eliyu Guldin proposes, in descending order, the following scheme for rural China (2001, 264–65). High status: (1) leading party and government cadres; (2) managers of large-scale, nonprivate enterprises; (3) large-scale private entrepreneurs with a locally significant financial power. Upper-medium status: (4) other cadres; (5) professionals; (6) other large-scale private entrepreneurs; (7) managers of small-scale enterprises. Lower-medium status: (8) employees of collective enterprises, (9) private small-scale entrepreneurs. Low status: (10) contract workers in collective enterprises (other than migrant workers); (11) laborers working in private enterprises; (12) small peasants; (13) migrant workers.

3. As regards these statistics on employment, Marton (2000) observes: "While the absolute number of rural workers included a small proportion who have moved to work in urban areas (especially in construction), the official statistics conceal the fact that there was much occupational overlap and dual employment. Many of those employed primarily in agriculture, for example, spent at least part of their working time engaged in non-agricultural activities. More significant was the fact that the rural workers were frequently released from the factories and other non-agricultural activities during the particularly busy stages of cultivation" (77).

4. For comparison, in 1980 the Melbourne, Philadelphia, Los Angeles, and Caracas metropolitan areas had overall population densities of, respectively, 468, 516, 709, and 1,073 people per square kilometer (Corporació Metropolitana de Barcelona, 1986).

5. A similar strategy was proposed by John Friedmann and Mike Douglass in a conference paper presented in Nagoya in 1975, and subsequently reprinted in a volume edited by Fu-chen Lo and Kamal Salih. The objective was "to transform the countryside by introducing and adapting elements of urbanism to specific rural settings. This means: instead of encouraging the drift of rural people to cities by investing in cities, encouraging them to remain where they are by investing in rural districts, and so transmute existing settlements into a hybrid form we call *agropolis* or city-in-the-fields. In agropolitan development the age-old conflict between town and countryside can be transcended" (Friedmann and Douglass 1978, 183). The model spelled out in this article is a virtual map to *in situ* urbanization actually carried out in China's coastal regions in the 1980s and beyond.

6. For a detailed historical account of various craft traditions in China, see Xu and Wu 2000.

7. In an interesting aside, Jonathan Unger suggests that despite political upheavals, certain habits, cultural skills, and attitudes may be passed down through the generations. "Even in large agricultural districts," he writes, "success in local specialization or in farming often seems to be related to family know-how that was handed down through the generations or, alternatively, to prior personal work experience: a tractor driver or auto mechanic under the collectives held definite advantages when it came to earning money privately in the post-Mao rural transport industry" (2002, 136–37).

8. Chi Fusheng had started life as a farmer. Before becoming general manager of the collective and head of the village (now township) government, he had completed six years of education. In the past, he had been the secretary of the village and had also served as a militia team leader (Hoffman and Liu 1997, n. 13). In a country where much of the rural population was functionally illiterate, a middle-school education apparently helped propel Chi to a top position in his village. But he was also a man with vision and considerable managerial talent.

9. In light of earlier discussion of historical antecedents, the following observation is of interest. In their study of development in Hangzhou and Wenzhou, Forster and Yao (1999) point to the city's traditional emphasis on profits and respect for commerce, "a countervailing cultural tradition to mainstream Confucian values. . . . During the southern Song dynasty, a school of learning emerged in Wenzhou known as the Yongjia school. It criticized the hegemonic Confucian value system and proposed more attention to industry, commerce and profit in order to enrich the country. . . . At the end of the nineteenth century three local scholars, known as the 'three gentlemen of Dong Ou' (East Wenzhou), reiterated this basic position. This distinctive cultural and ideological tradition has provided a basis for the entrepreneurial spirit of the people of Wenzhou, which has served them well in the reform period" (67).

10. Nomination procedures vary from village to village. Sometimes nominations are made by the party, at other times by village elders. Or hamlets (natural villages)

nominate their own candidates, while elections are villagewide. Or, as in one village, each voter could nominate their own candidate, whose name would then be publicized and voted upon, with the top five vote-getters becoming the official nominees (in this particular case, they were the three hamlet heads, the incumbent village head, and the village accountant) (Unger 2002, 218–22).

11. For a discussion of "amphibious institutions" in China, see chapter 6. The concept refers to the lack of clear boundaries between public, private, and collective institutions and their ability to assume different roles at different times without seeing in this any cause for concern.

12. "The electoral process is creeping upward out of the villages," writes Jonathan Unger. "The level of rural administration that most alienates many farmers is the township level. It appears to them to be the source for most local fees, taxes and fines. Village-level elections cannot assuage peasant discontent against township leaders; so if the process of electing officials at the lower level proves successful in restoring farmers' goodwill, why not attempt elections for rural township leaders? Even some of the top leaders in Beijing are enticed by such a notion" (2002, 221–22). For a more detailed discussion of this issue, see Saich and Yang 2003.

13. Once a village is urbanized administratively, it loses the right to formally elect its own government, the village (now urban neighborhood) committee.

14. This account of rural urbanization in Quanzhou dovetails with a more detailed study of *chengzhongcun* in Guangzhou, complemented with national survey data for the late 1990s (Zhang, Zhao, and Tian 2003). *Chengzhongcun* is a general term for a residential concentration of migrants who are low-income and are denied access to low-cost state housing. Most of these concentrations are found in peri-urban villages, though a large number are also found inside the metropolitan core. According to the Guangzhou survey, most migrants are satisfied with their housing conditions, despite the very dense occupancy rate. "A substantial number of dwellings have essential facilities like tap water, electricity, private kitchens, flush toilets and sewage drainage that offer better living conditions than many distant and isolated rural areas" (923). Nevertheless, the authors assert that "to some extent, . . . the *chengzhongcun* resemble some of the worst features of shanty towns in other cities of the world" (924). This may be too harsh a judgment. Shantytowns elsewhere in the world are self-built in a very different way; they tend to be lean-tos constructed by the residents themselves from found materials. Individual housing may or may not be consolidated over time, and squatter areas may eventually be absorbed into the urban grid once land use is regularized and infrastructure facilities are extended to them. The entire process is very different from the one described either by Anderson or the authors of the Guangzhou study. For more details on migrant housing, see the next chapter.

15. Community development is an approach dear to the hearts of anthropologists, sociologists, and the voluntary sector. It is a strategy of what is delicately called poverty alleviation and is applied precisely in places where economic development

has not been occurring. Community development specialists work with local inhabitants to identify so-called community needs, such as water supply and drainage, and to help mobilize the community to build the necessary facilities with their own hands, sometimes with outside material assistance. Community development of this sort has been widely applied in India, Pakistan, and Africa south of the Sahara.

4. NEW SPATIAL MOBILITIES

1. Nor was it always rigorously enforced or rather, different parts of the central state were sometimes working at cross-purposes. As Cheng and Selden report, "Ironically, from 1958, as the state tried to enforce rigorous measures to bind cultivators to the land and particularly to block urban immigration and reduce the population of large cities, the number of urban migrants increased dramatically. Population movement reached a peak at the height of the Great Leap Forward. In contrast to the utopian production figures touted at the time, *this* was not a case of fabricated numbers. The twin explanations for this paradoxical outcome lie, first, in the fact that the state's priority at this time was not population control but accelerated development. The tough new restrictions were simply swept aside as enterprises, including many urban factories, stepped up recruitment of workers. Moreover, at the very moment when new laws expanded the reach of the state, the decentralization and chaos of the leap produced a general breakdown of administrative control" (1994, 665).

2. According to Wang Feng, as of 1993 nearly two-thirds of China's population lived within administrative municipalities and, according to this ample definition, can be defined as "urban." The percentage of nonagricultural *hukou* in this understanding of "urban" was only 32 percent, however, leaving the great majority with an agricultural residence permit irrespective of the activities they were actually engaged in. A narrower definition puts the figure of urban population in 1993 at 29 percent, of whom only 27 percent have a rural *hukou* (Wang 1997, 154, table 1).

3. Mallee points out that migration tends to be a household rather than individual decision. We may add that both the volume of migration and the time spent away from home are variable. These variables are likely to depend on prior household experiences with migration, the likelihood of finding a job in a specific location (very few migrants set out without knowing where they are headed), and general economic conditions in the country. Poor rural households cannot maintain migrants to distant cities for extended periods of time while they are searching for paid work.

4. According to data in Zhang, Zhao, and Tian (2003), migrant occupations in a 1995 survey were distributed as follows: managerial and technical staff, 1.0 percent; skilled workers, 22.5 percent; production workers, 68.0 percent; and supporting workers, 8.5 percent (table 2). In their own survey of *chenzhongcun* (conducted in 1999) they discovered a highly skewed educational profile for migrants: 71 percent of their sample of 459 migrants had completed secondary and high school education, and 10 percent had at least some university education (table 4). Nevertheless, most migrants are

employed in the informal sector on a temporary basis. "They take whatever job is available to them. Because many of these jobs are of a temporary nature, few migrants stick to only a single job. A handful of self-employed are, in fact, small vendors and craftsmen. The remarkable diversity in origin and jobs reflects the complicated pattern of migrant enclaves in today's China" (921).

5. The basis for this estimate is not clear. In principle, agricultural labor is labeled "surplus" if the same total output from the sector could be produced without those workers. Such calculations, however, are highly speculative and are built on questionable assumptions.

6. Li Zhang (2001, 129) reports that some migrant bosses from Wenzhou in Beijing's Zhejiang village who employ migrant women from other provinces in their home workshops may withhold payments for up to a year.

7. Anderson (2003, 50) reports: "Some rent shops in the village or industrial parks servicing factory workers. Types of shops include restaurants, clothing and shoe stores, mobile phone and long-distance phone centers, hairdressers, bicycle repair shops, household goods shops, and corner stores selling cigarettes, soda pop, and other small items. Shopkeepers say that generally once they have paid rent on their shops they do not make any more money than they did as factory workers (which is how most of them started off), but that running a shop is easier. . . . Other small businesses set up on the street, including fruit sellers who push carts or carry baskets on a pole, tailors or shoe repair people, or sellers of CDs and tapes, books, hair accessories or other small items."

8. Zhang, Zhao, and Tian (2003, table 5) present 1999 survey data from Guangzhou that provide an interesting contrast. Sampling 455 migrants, they found that the average monthly income was 1,028 yuan compared to 267 yuan before migration. Monthly savings were 425 yuan, of which 347 yuan was remitted back home. But these averages hide the actual distribution of incomes. After migration, 22 percent of the migrants sampled earned less than 500 yuan a month, of which a substantial amount went toward food and lodging. Savings and remittances were correspondingly less.

9. In their study of migrant housing, Zhang, Zhao, and Tian (2003) observe: "although migrant settlements in Chinese cities are often formed by people originating from the same place and are better known for producing one or two specialized products, not all *chengzhongcun* are necessarily ethnically based and employment-specialized. . . . We found that many *chengzhaocun*, as migrant enclaves, were in fact loosely structured socially, lacking dominant ethnic connections such as in Zhejiang village and Wenzhou village in Beijing" (919).

10. By convention, linguistic differences in China are usually referred to as dialects. But many of them are mutually incomprehensible, just as in Western Europe, Dutch or Swiss German are considered separate languages rather than dialects. These differences are intensified among peasant communities where each valley may speak its own local "dialect."

11. For a book-length study of return migration, see Murphy 2002a.

12. According to United Nations estimates, the proportion of population resid-ing in urban areas in China will increase from 40.6 percent in 2000 to 50.8 percent by 2015 and 59.1 percent by 2030 (United Nations Department of Economic and Social Affairs 1998, table A.2). Most of these projected increases are no doubt a result of migration.

13. A more radical, provincial-level strategy for attracting in-bound investments is reported for Sichuan by Lijian Hong (1999). It is called the "boat-borrowing" pol-icy. According to this policy, writes Hong, "local enterprises were encouraged to set up 'window enterprises' in China's coastal regions, especially in the special economic zones (SEZs) in order to exploit the benefits of the preferential policies granted to the SEZs, and to share the fast economic growth in China's coastal regions. The most important part of the policy was that once these window enterprises were estab-lished, they were allowed to invest back into Sichuan. As enterprises from the SEZs, these window enterprises were entitled to enjoy special tax exemptions. By the end of 1990, Sichuan had established more than 700 window enterprises . . . [and] RMB 30 million was sent back to Sichuan" (197).

5. EXPANDING SPACES OF PERSONAL AUTONOMY

1. In his excellent ethnography of a rural village in China's northernmost pro-vince, Heilongjiang, Yan (2003) arrives at similar conclusions. The village has no indus-tries; its principal crop is maize. It is a poor village, and during the collectivist era it had a kind of public life in which everyone in the village took part, albeit under the guidance of party officials. With the dissolution of the commune system, people with-drew from public life, retreating into the privacy of their own homes, where they spent many hours in front of newly acquired television sets, participating vicariously in the wider world beyond their village. At the same time, life had become less inter-esting for many; in fact, many resisted the "responsibility" system of farming, though, of course, it was implemented in the end. This withdrawal from public life was accompanied by many other changes, including a greater sense of personal autonomy (especially among the younger generation), an acute sense of privacy, and new courtship patterns. All these trends would be replicated in intensified form in China's large cities.

2. For good recent collections of essays on everyday life in urban China, see Weston and Jensen 2000; Davis 2000; Chen et al. 2001; and Link, Madsen, and Pickowicz 2002.

3. In this section, I will not deal with the erosion of the residential permit sys-tem, which made possible the migratory movement of tens of millions of workers to urban areas. For details see chapter 4.

4. Tomba (2004) brings these statistics up to date. The State Council in May 1995 introduced a compulsory five-day working week, with the explicit intention of

increasing consumer spending. Tomba further reports that, "according to a recent study carried out in three major cities, the average amount of leisure time available to urban employees has already surpassed actual working time" (10–11). But, he adds, "those who have been given the greatest number of days of leisure time happen to be skilled employees (in the cultural, health, research and education sectors) as well as Party cadres" (11). As we saw in chapter 4, however, increased leisure was not available to migrant workers in the peri-urban areas of China's coastal cities. They might work twelve-hour days for days on end without time off and were lucky to get paid at all.

5. Davis's data are for urban *hukou* holders only. Migrant housing conditions were, of course, different. According to a national survey carried out by the Ministry of Public Security in 1999, 16.1 percent of migrants lived in self-built shelters on construction sites; 31.1 percent lived in rented quarters; 29.6 percent lived in dormitories provided by employers; 10.2 percent lived with relatives and friends; and 9.2 percent lived in hostels (Zhang, Zhao, and Tian 2003, table 6). Living conditions for migrants are infinitely more crowded than they are for urban residents, and most migrants, even though they may be married, come to the city alone, leaving their familiies behind in their home villages (and towns).

6. These findings are confirmed by the 2000 census. According to Wang (2003, 137), "housing space for urban households reached 25 square meters per person in the year 2000. Such a number suggests a close to three-fold increase in housing space in two decades." In that same year, nearly three-quarters of urban households were reported to own their housing units. If correct, this is an incredible achievement. At the same time, an index of housing inequality in terms of space per capita has overtaken the Gini coefficient for income.

7. *Qigong* is a spiritual practice as well as a martial art, a healing ritual, and a meditation practice. A form of *qigong* familiar to Westerners is *tai-qi* (*tai-chi*). The spiritual movement of Falun Gong belongs to this same category, though it appears to have become politicized and since 1999 has been suppressed by the state as an "evil cult."

8. For an excellent review of China's urban consumer revolution, see Davis 2000. The upwardly mobile consumer class of China's big cities is at the present time probably not much larger than 10 percent of urban population.

9. "The notion of the state as an ally in furthering and protecting individuals' economic rights is not, of course, unique to China," writes Hooper (2000). "Within a broader developmental context, this alliance has been characteristic of a number of countries during the early phase of economic development: from Korea and Taiwan to Thailand and Malaysia. As individuals benefit from economic development and constitute a nascent 'middle class,' they represent a set of social interests which seek protection by law of their rising living standards and expanding consumption" (127).

10. As reported by Hooper (2000), "While the Internet is still in its relative infancy in China, it has grown exponentially, from an estimated 670,000 users at the

beginning of 1998 to almost nine million at the end of 1999, with numbers now estimated to be doubling every six months" (105). The latest available figures are for the
end of 2001, when the number of users had grown to 33.7 million (Giese 2003, 31).

11. I deliberately use the term *liberty* in this connection to remind us that they
are politically embedded rather than natural phenomena given to us at birth.

12. The liveliness of political intellectual discourse in China, especially during
the latter part of the 1990s, is quite surprising to those who don't read Chinese. The
controversies at that time were between the neo-liberals and neo-socialists whose
polemics were chiefly directed at an academic audience (see Bonnin and Chevrier
1996; Barmé 2000). Given this intellectual climate, a seemingly moderate "reformer,"
such as Liao Xun, who has a clear-cut, practical program of how to translate new
political ideas into practice, may actually end up getting a promotion!

13. Yang (1997, 31) refers to Hainan Province as "the most radical experiment in
the preferential politics of regional development."

14. See, for example, Joseph Y. H. Cheng (2000), who writes: "Redefining government functions has been viewed both as a prerequisite and a logical consequence
of . . . reforms of state enterprises. The thrust of economic restructuring has thus
been separating government from enterprises and the promotion of 'small government, big society.' The latter implies that governments at all levels should limit their
functions and allow people to acquire the good and services they want from the
market" (12).

15. Gold 1990; Wakeman 1993; Huang 1993, Gu 1993–94; Ding 1994; White,
Howell, and Shang 1996; Brook and Frolic 1997; Chamberlain 1998; Pei 1998; Cheek
1998.

16. The term *individual* has a resonance in Anglo-American society that it does
not have in Chinese, where individuals understand themselves as knotted into a web
of personal relationships with kin and others. As Pye (1996) comments, "it still remains
true that the dominant feature of Confucianism was a pervasive hostility to the notion
of personal autonomy and individualism. The goal of self-improvement was moral perfection according to established standards, and hence it sought excellence in terms of
conformity to cultural norms, not in terms of the uniqueness of each individual.
There was a hierarchy of moral achievement in which only the elite could strive for
self-development while the mass of the people were ruled by example. Above all,
however, there was no notion of individual rights" (19–20). But recourse to Confucian
values to explain personal conduct in today's China may have limited validity. Today's
individual, according to Yan (2003), has become distinctly "uncivil" and egocentric.

17. For an idealistic account of Greek democracy, see Arendt (1958).

6. THE GOVERNANCE OF CITY-BUILDING

1. This statement is disputed by Rozman (2003, 181) who argues that "decentralization," in the sense of greater autonomy at the local sphere, is a fundamental ideal

of Confucianism, though not an explicit tenet. He understands localism as a balance to, or check on, centralism. In other words, he finds principles of good governance in the Confucian tradition. Rozman believes that economic dynamism has its origins in local social relations, and that the center should provide moral guidance but should not control decisions hierarchically. "It is time," he writes, "to make the implicit Confucian acceptance of localism an explicit statement about the role of community as defender of tradition. The Confucian element is strong encouragement for local identity and initiative, as the central state clears away obstacles to individual and family strategies for educational, entrepreneurial, and knowledge-based success" (198). Such views, however, are not widely shared in present-day China.

2. "It is clear," writes Mote (1999), "that the Chinese government [in the Ming dynasty] and the people themselves expected local government to be accomplished in large part by the prevailing and commonly accepted standards of social behavior, that is by the normative controls built into the shared culture of all the people" (952). For the classical debates, see Graham 1989. Legalist doctrine, carried to an extreme by the First Emperor, is discussed by Jullien (1995) in the following terms: "To strive for morality is . . . harmful, and those who preach morality are corrupt, since it introduces slackness into what would otherwise run tightly on its own. The only correct way to use the sovereign's position is to recognize that it works *automatically*. One with such a system at his disposal, far from drawing attention to himself by his favors, like the Confucian king, conceals himself within its machinery, becoming indistinguishable from its cogs. He who is all-seeing offers no glimpse of himself, forcing transparency on others but protecting himself through his own opacity" (53–54). To a modern Western historian, this remark is suggestive of the eighteenth-century British liberal reformer Jeremy Bentham, who invented the panopticon, a prison where the prisoners are seen from a central location, but never the observer.

3. Creel (1974) comments on the work of the fourth-century philosopher Shen Pu-Hai, "he seems to have been the first to articulate the idea that for government virtue is not enough—that there must be techniques clearly understood, formulated, and studied. This was a debate that would continue throughout history" (290).

4. "Primitive accumulation [wrote Marx] is not the result of the capitalist mode of production but its starting point" (Tucker 1978, 431). Marx called it a process that is "anything but idyllic" (432).

5. This description of administrative levels is somewhat stylized. For a more nuanced discussion, see Skinner 1977a, 301–7.

6. In this way, they were quite unlike European cities with their corporate identity and, particularly in northern Europe and the Mediterranean region, a tradition of powerful city-states, such as the cities of the Hanseatic League in the north and Venice, Genoa, and other cities in the south.

7. As the American poet Gertrude Stein is supposed to have said of the city of Oakland, California, "there is no there there." Min (2002) seems to be arguing that

something like a collective self-identity emerged in Suzhou during the first decade of the twentieth century, but even he stops short of claiming self-governance for the city.

8. The photo graces the dustjacket of Skinner, ed., 1977. It is also reproduced in Strand (1989, 76) where it is identified as "the outer city from Qian Gate." Strand claims to see only six policemen.

9. For details, see the excellent case studies collected in Esherick 1999.

10. For a fascinating perspective on the history of the National People's Congress (NPC) and its provincial and local clones, see Potter 2003. Also relevant here is the recent controversial assessment of the NPC by Dowdle 2002.

11. The head of a Shanghai Residents' Committee makes the following comment on the tensions between his committee and the new Property Owners' Association (POA). "Our neighborhood is managed by three separate institution: the Residents' Committee (RC), the POA, and a property management company paid by the POA. The RC has responsibility to the district government and receives various public tasks from the district, but with no power to do business. The POA collects money and can do whatever it wants with the money. The property management company was previously the local branch of the housing bureau but is financially independent. It is the real manager of local business but with no responsibility to the government. It collects management fees but does little. We [the RC] do all the work given by the government but with no money. Our office budget is only 250 yuan ($30) per month, and this little money can do nothing but pay for the telephone" (Zhang 2002b, 318).

12. Unlike the situation in the United States, real estate companies and developers are not necessarily in private hands but are frequently and in various ways off-shoots from the local government. Such organizations have been referred to as "amphibious."

13. To speak of the existence of a land market in China is somewhat misleading. Much the larger part of land use rights is administratively transferred to *danwei* for only a nominal fee. Work units, in turn, have become major housing developers. In Shanghai, for example, they accounted for 86 percent of total housing investment in 1990. As Zhou and Logan (1996) observe, "Work unit housing and cooperative housing were considered a transitional step in market housing reform, the next phase was to press for the creation of a private housing market. This was a politically difficult move. It faced potential resistance from all social strata. . . . As a result, although overall housing conditions for urban workers have been significantly improved by investment, the distribution of commodified housing is similar to the old system, except that housing is no longer free" (415–16). Work units, of course, stand to make enormous profits from such transactions.

14. This account is also applicable to land use rights put up by *danwei* and collectively held village land. However, it is illegal to sell administratively allocated land without the government's permission and the payment of a land premium. (I am grateful to Professor M. K. Ng for this information.)

15. The central government is also concerned with controlling rampant land speculation. In 1994 the City Real Estate Management Act became law. At the same time, "the State Council asked local government to tighten up company registration. Development zones without proper approval were shut down. A transaction tax was levied on the transfer of use rights without substantial development. Developers also had to turn in a value-added tax if they obtained windfall profits from the land" (Yeh and Wu 1998, 222). Since 2002, Land Management Centers have been established in each city, and municipal land is now leased at public auction. The hope is that this new process will reduce the opportunities for corruption (Cao Dawei, personal communication).

16. It might be well, however, to put China's reputation for excessive corruption in a global perspective. A German nonprofit organization based in Berlin, Transparency International, tracks corruption worldwide. In its 2002 Corruption Perceptions Index, which is based on multiple surveys for each country, China ranks 58th out of a total of 102 countries. Finland stands in first place, Bangladesh in last. Some comparative rank-order places are instructive: Singapore, 5; Hong Kong, 14; United States, 16; Japan, 20; Taiwan, 29; Italy, 31; Brazil, 45; India, 71; Russia, 71; Indonesia, 96. See the organization's Web site: www.transparency.org/cpi/2002/cpi2002.en.hmtl. Useful as these benchmarks are, one should not put too much stock in these rankings. For example, at the level of local transactions, the dividing line between what is corrupt, traditional *guanxi*, and legal practice is not always clearly drawn, and people seem to have considerable tolerance for small-time graft. The matter is more serious, of course, when corruption reaches into the higher levels of the state bureaucracy and party. As Pye (1996) observes, "Objectively measured, the level of corruption may not be much worse than is the norm for third world countries, but subjective legitimacy in China is still tied to the idea that the government should be the defender of a moral order. Therefore, if there is a decline in moral standards, the state is directly at fault" (35).

17. For a similar analysis, but from a very different perspective, see Rocca 2003. This French scholar speaks of the "statification of society" and the "societalization of the state." Both terms are precisely descriptive but unwieldy. In his view, it is this interpenetration of state and society that lends the system of governance in China considerable stability.

18. For details, see Yeh and Wu 1998, chapter 2. The City Planning Act was preceded by the City Planning Ordinance issued by the State Council in 1984. "Through this state directive," write Abramson, Leaf, and Ying (2002), "all municipal and county governments were required to develop master plans to guide their physical development in accordance with existing practices of local economic planning" (167).

19. A licensing exam for professional planners tests candidates on their knowledge of planning principles, planning laws and regulations, planning ethics, and professional practice (Zhang 2002a).

20. Guangzhou's current population, including temporary workers, is estimated

at around 6 million. This discrepancy suggests that much of the planning—geared to an invariant population in possession of an urban *hukou* of half that size—is completely unrealistic. More recently, so-called temporary population estimates have been added to calculate space requirements, though at a ratio of only two-thirds of the space requirements for urban *hukou* holders.

21. Or in Guangzhou: remember the 3 million uncounted population, many of them considered mere "floaters" who have no rights to the city at all.

22. For excellent case studies of planning in Quanzhou, see Abramson, Leaf, and Ying 2002; Leaf and Abramson 2002. For Shenzhen, see Ng and Tang 2002.

23. See note 2.

CONCLUSION

1. To be fair, Jiang Zemin's thesis of the "Three Represents" avoids any reference to the Leninist vanguard role of the party. In this theory, the party's role is to represent the development trend of China's *advanced productive forces*, the orientation of China's *advanced culture,* and the fundamental interests of the *overwhelming majority of the Chinese people*. The precise meaning of this pronouncement is, of course, open to various interpretations.

2. The project was funded by the U.K. Economic and Social Research Council and the Wuhan Environmental Protection Bureau.

3. For an excellent study of implementing pollution control in Sichuan, with comparisons to eastern provinces, see van Rooij (2003). Although an administrative system is now in place to enforce regulations with regard to air and water pollution, and steady progress has been made over the past few years in the control of pollution, the present system is far from adequate. In a simple enforcement ratio for the year 2000 (enforcement cases related to 10,000 tons of major pollution indicators), van Rooij shows that the best performer was Jiangsu Province with a ratio of 22.4, while Sichuan ranked at the bottom with a ratio of 1.6. The average for China as a whole was 7.3 (ibid., table 4).

4. The serious impacts the uncontrolled use of the private automobile may have on Chinese cities is discussed in a first-rate paper by Kenworthy and Hu (2002).

5. For another case study, see Abramson, Leaf, and Ying 2002.

6. According to Khan and Riskin (2001), unemployment stood at 8.5 percent of the urban labor force in the mid-1990s. This estimate is based on a sample study in nine provinces. Unemployment is a very fuzzy concept, however, and estimates depend entirely on the definition of both "unemployment" and "labor force." Besides, under present conditions, the category "employed person" might include anyone who has joined the street economy of the informal sector, regardless of earnings. According to Solinger (2003, 69), there are forty thousand pedicab drivers in Wuhan who used to have regular jobs in SOEs and who now barely eke out a living, much as did the rickshaw pullers in Beijing during the 1920s.

7. Poverty, like unemployment, is a difficult concept to measure, and definitions can always be challenged. In the Khan and Riskin study, the headcount index was constructed by estimating the minimum daily caloric requirement for an urban worker, and translating the cost of these calories into the purchasing power required to buy them in food-equivalent terms on the market. With the cost of food amounting to 55 percent of all expenditures, a poverty threshold of 2,291 yuan per year (191 yuan per month) was calculated. Intermediate and low poverty thresholds were then put at 80 percent and 70 percent, respectively (Khan and Riskin 2001, 79–80).

8. The urban sustainability problems I have briefly identified are by no means the only ones with which cities have to be concerned. There is also the matter of land conversion, as highly productive agricultural lands are changed to urban uses; the very serious water problems encountered particularly in the northeastern cities, where ground water tables are falling precipitously; the creeping desertification of lands due to overgrazing, which gives rise to periodic dust storms blowing sand over northeastern cities; the continuing serious problems of air and water pollution; and the high social costs imposed by the increasing use of automobiles. For details see Smil 1993; Sinkule and Ortolano 1995; Ho and Kueh 2000; Kenworthy and Hu 2002; Brown 2003; and Ho and Lin 2004.

References

Abramson, Daniel B., Michael Leaf, and Tan Ying. 2002. "Social Research and the Localization of Chinese Urban Planning Practice: Some Ideas from Quanzhou, Fujian." In John R. Logan, ed., *The New Chinese City: Globalization and Market Reform*, 167–80. Oxford: Blackwell.

Abu-Lughod, Janet. 1989. *Before European Hegemony: The World System A.D. 1250–1350*. New York: Oxford University Press.

Anderson, Samantha. 2003. "Cities on the Edge: Peri-Urbanization in South-eastern China." Master's thesis, School of Community and Regional Planning, University of British Columbia, Vancouver, Canada.

Arendt, Hannah. 1958. *The Human Condition*. Chicago: University of Chicago Press.

Barmé, Geremie R. 2000. "The Revolution of Resistance." In Elizabeth J. Perry and Mark Selden, eds., *Chinese Society: Change, Conflict, Resistance*, 198–220. London: Routledge.

Bøkman, Harald. 1998. "China Deconstructs? The Future of the Chinese Empire-State in a Historical Perspective." In Kjeld Erik Brødsgaard and David Strand, eds., *Reconstructing Twentieth Century China: State Control, Civil Society, and National Culture*, 310–46. Oxford: Clarendon Press.

Bonnin, Michel, and Yves Chevrier. 1996. "The Intellectual and the State: Social Dynamics of Intellectual Autonomy during the Post-Mao Era." In Brian Hook, ed., *The Individual and the State in China*, 149–74. Oxford: Clarendon Press.

Braudel, Fernand. 1992. *The Perspective of the World*. Vol. 3 of *Civilization and Capitalism*. Berkeley: University of California Press.

Brødsgaard, Kjeld Erik. 1998. "State and Society in Hainan: Liao Xun's Ideas on 'Small Government, Big Society.'" In Kjeld Erik Brødsgaard and David Strand, eds., *Reconstructing Twentieth Century China: State Control, Civil Society, and National Culture*, 189–215. Oxford: Clarendon Press.

Brook, Timothy. 1997. "Auto-Organization in Chinese Society." In Timothy Brook and B. Michael Frolic, eds., *Civil Society in China*, 19–45. Armonk, N.Y.: M. E. Sharpe.

Brook, Timothy, and B. Michael Frolic, eds.1997. *Civil Society in China.* Armonk, N.Y.: M. E. Sharpe.

Brosseau, Maurice. 1998. "Entrepreneurs Probing Uncertainty and Bounded Rationality." In Y. M. Yeung and David K. Y. Chu, eds., *Guangdong: Survey of a Province Undergoing Rapid Change,* 191–232. 2d ed. Hong Kong: Chinese University Press.

Brown, Lester R. 2003. *Plan B: Rescuing a Planet under Stress and a Civilization in Trouble.* New York: W. W. Norton.

Castells, Manuel. 1996. *The Rise of the Network Society.* Oxford: Blackwell Publishers.

Chamberlain, Heath. 1998. "Civil Society with Chinese Characteristics." *China Journal* 39 (January): 69–82.

Chan, Anita. 2002. "The Culture of Survival: Lives of Migrant Workers through the Prism of Private Letters." In Perry Link, Richard P. Madsen, and Paul G. Pickowicz, eds., *Popular China: Unofficial Culture in a Globalizing Society,* 163–88. Lanham, Md.: Rowman and Littlefield.

Chan, Kam Wing. 1994. *Cities with Invisible Walls: Reinterpreting Urbanization in Post-1949 China.* Hong Kong: Oxford University Press.

Chan, Kam Wing, and Yong Hu. 2003. "Urbanization in China in the 1990s: New Definition, Different Series, and Revised Trends." *China Review* 3, no. 2.

Cheek, Timothy. 1998. "From Market to Democracy in China: Gaps in the Civil Society Model." In Juan D. Lindau and Timothy Cheek, eds., *Market Economics and Political Change: Comparing China and Mexico,* 219–54. Lanham, Md.: Rowman and Littlefield.

Chen, Nancy N. 1995. "Urban Spaces and Experiences of *Qigong.*" In Deborah S. Davis et al., eds., *Urban Spaces in Contemporary China: The Potential for Autonomy and Community in Post-Mao China,* 347–61. Washington, D.C.: Woodrow Wilson Center Press and Cambridge University Press.

Chen, Nancy N., et al., eds. 2001. *China Urban: Ethnographies of Contemporary Culture.* Durham, N.C.: Duke University Press.

Cheng, Joseph Y. S. 2000. "Guangdong's Challenges: Organizational Streamlining, Economic Restructuring, and Anticorruption." *Pacific Affairs* 73, no. 1 (Spring): 9–36.

Cheng, Tiejun, and Mark Selden. 1994. "The Origins and Social Consequences of China's *Hukou* System." *China Quarterly* 139: 644–68.

Cheung, Peter T. Y. 1998. "Changing Relations between the Central Government and Guangdong." In Y. M. Yeung and David K. Y. Chu, eds., *Guandong: Survey of a Province Undergoing Rapid Change,* 23–62. 2d ed. Hong Kong: Chinese University Press.

———. 2002. "Managing the Hong Kong–Guandong Relationship." In Anthony Gai-on Yeh et al., eds., *Building a Competitive Pearl River Delta Region,* 39–56. Hong Kong: Centre of Urban Planning and Environmental Management, University of Hong Kong.

Commission on Strategic Development. 2000. *Bringing the Vision to Life: Hong Kong's Long-term Development Needs and Goals.* February.

Corporació Metropolitana de Barcelona. 1986. *Giant Cities of the World.* Publication prepared by the scientific commission of the Spanish Task Force of the International Conference on Population and the Urban Future. Barcelona: Corporació Metropolitana.

Creel, Herrlee G. 1974. *Shen Pu-Hai: A Chinese Political Philosopher of the Fourth Century B.C.* Chicago: University of Chicago Press.

Davis, Deborah S. 2002. "When a House Becomes His Home." In Perry Link, Richard P. Madsen, and Paul G. Pickowicz, eds., *Popular China: Unofficial Culture in a Globalizing Society,* 231–50. Lanham, Md.: Rowman and Littlefield.

———, ed. 2000. *China's Urban Consumer Revolution.* Berkeley: University of California Press.

Des Forges, Roger V. 1997. "States, Society, and Civil Societies in Chinese History." In Timothy Brook and B. Michael Frolic, eds., *Civil Society in China,* 68–95. Armonk, N.Y.: M. E. Sharpe.

De Tocqueville, Alexis. 1969. *Democracy in America.* New York: Doubleday.

DiGregorio, Michael R. 2001. "Iron Works: Excavating Alternative Futures in a Northern Vietnamese Craft Village." Ph.D. diss., University of California, Los Angeles.

Ding, X. L. 1994. "Institutional Amphibiousness and the Transition from Communism: The Case of China." *British Journal of Political Science* 24, no. 1: 293–318.

Douglass, Mike, and John Friedmann, eds. 1998. *Cities for Citizens: Planning and the Rise of Civil Society in a Global Age.* Chichester, N.Y.: John Wiley and Sons.

Dowdle, Michael William. 2002. "Constructing Citizenship: The NPC as Catalyst for Political Participation." In Merle Goldman and Elizabeth J. Perry, eds., *Changing Meanings of Citizenship in Modern China,* 330–49. Cambridge, Mass.: Harvard University Press.

Elvin, Mark. 1974. "Introduction." In Mark Elvin and G. William Skinner, eds., *The Chinese City between Two Worlds,* 1–16. Stanford, Calif.: Stanford University Press.

Erwin, Kathleen. 2000. "Heart-to-Heart, Phone-to-Phone: Family Values, Sexuality, and the Politics of Shanghai's Advice Hotlines." In Deborah S. Davis, ed., *China's Urban Consumer Revolution,* 145–70. Berkeley: University of California Press.

Esherick, Joseph W., ed. 1999. *Remaking the Chinese City: Modernity and National Identity, 1900–1950.* Honolulu: University of Hawai'i Press.

Fairbank, John King. 1986. *The Great Chinese Revolution: 1800–1985.* New York: Harper and Row.

Fan, Cindy C. 1997. "Uneven Development and Beyond: Regional Development Theory in Post-Mao China." *International Journal for Urban and Regional Research* 21: 620–39.

Far Eastern Economic Review. 2003a. "The Angry Face behind the Real Estate Bonanza." June 19: 31.

———. 2003b. "Untying the Knot." September 11: 30–31.

Faure, David, and Tao Tao Liu, eds. 2002. *Town and Country in China: Identity and Perception.* New York: Palgrave.

Feiner, Jacques, Diego Salmerón, Ernst Joos, and Willy A. Schmid. 2002. "Priming Sustainability: The Kunming Urban Region Development Project." *DISP* 151 (Zurich), 38, no. 4: 59–67.

Forster, Keith, and Xianguo Yao. 1999. "A Comparative Analysis of Economic Reform and Development in Hangzhou and Wenzhou Cities." In Jae Hung Chung, ed., *Cities in China: Recipes for Economic Development in the Reform Era,* 53–104. London: Routledge.

Friedmann, John. 1986. "The World City Hypothesis." *Development and Change* 17, no. 1: 69–84.

———. 1998a. "The New Political Economy of Planning: The Rise of Civil Society." In Mike Douglass and John Friedmann, eds., *Cities for Citizens: Planning and the Rise of Civil Society in a Global Age,* 19–35. Chichester, N.Y.: John Wiley and Sons.

———. 1998b. "World City Futures: The Role of Urban and Regional Policies in the Asia-Pacific Region." In Yue-man Yeung, ed., *Urban Development and Asia: Retrospect and Prospect,* 25–44. Hong Kong: Chinese University Press.

———. 2002. *The Prospect of Cities.* Minneapolis: University of Minnesota Press.

Friedmann, John, and Mike Douglass. 1978. "Agropolitan Development: Towards a New Strategy for Regional Planning in Asia." In Fu-chen Lo and Kamal Salih, eds., *Growth Pole Strategy and Regional Development Policy: Asian Experiences and Alternative Approaches,* 147–62. Published for the United Nations Centre for Regional Development. Oxford: Pergamon Press.

Friedmann, John, and Clyde Weaver. 1979. *Territory and Function: The Evolution of Regional Planning.* Berkeley: University of California Press.

Gaubatz, Piper Rae. 1995. "Urban Transformation in Post-Mao China: Impacts of the Reform Era on China's Urban Form." In Deborah S. Davis et al., eds., *Urban Spaces in Contemporary China: The Potential for Autonomy and Community in Post-Mao China,* 28–60. Washington, D.C.: Woodrow Wilson Center Press and Cambridge University Press.

Gernet, Jacques. 1996. *A History of Chinese Civilization.* Translated by J. R. Foster and Charles Hartman. 2d ed. Cambridge: Cambridge University Press.

Giese, Karsten. 2003. "Internet Growth and the Digital Divide: Implications for Spatial Development." In Christopher Hughes and Gudrun Wacker, eds., *China and the Internet: Politics of the Digital Leap,* 30–57. London: Routledge Curzon.

Gilley, Bruce. 2004. "The 'End of Politics' in Beijing." *China Journal* 51: 115–35.

Gold, Thomas B. 1990. "The Resurgence of Civil Society in China." *Journal of Democracy* 1, no. 1 (Winter): 18–31.

Goldman, Merle, and Elizabeth J. Perry, eds. 2002. *Changing Meanings of Citizenship in Modern China.* Cambridge, Mass.: Harvard University Press.

Graham, A. C. 1989. *Disputers of the Tao: Philosophical Arguments in Ancient China.* La Salle, Ill.: Open Court.

Gu, Xin. 1993–94. "A Civil Society and Public Sphere in Post-Mao China? An Overview of Western Publications." *China Information* 8, no. 3 (Winter): 38–52.

Guldin, Gregory Eliyu. 2001. *What's a Peasant to Do? Village Becoming Town in Southern China.* Boulder, Colo.: Westview Press.

Guldin, Gregory Eliyu, ed. 1997. *Farewell to Peasant China: Rural Urbanization and Social Change in the Late Twentieth Century.* Armonk, N.Y.: M. E. Sharpe.

Habermas, Jürgen. 1989. *The Structural Transformation of the Public Sphere: An Inquiry into a Category of Bourgeois Society.* Translated by Thomas Burger with the assistance of Frederick Lawrence. Cambridge: Polity Press.

Heng, Chye Kiang. 1999. *Cities of Aristocrats and Bureaucrats: The Development of Medieval Chinese Cityscapes.* Singapore: National University of Singapore.

Ho, Samuel P. S., and Y. Y. Kueh. 2000. *Sustainable Economic Development in South China.* New York: St. Martin's Press.

Ho, Samuel P. S., and George C. S. Lin. 2004. "Converting Land to Nonagricultural Use in China's Coastal Provinces." *Modern China* 30, no. 1: 81–112.

Hoffman, Lis, and Zhongquan Liu. 1997. "Rural Urbanization on the Liaodong Peninsula: A Village, a Town, and a *Nonmin Chen.*" In Gregory Eliyu Guldin, ed., *Farewell to Peasant China: Rural Urbanization and Social Change in the Late Twentieth Century*. Armonk, N.Y.: M. E. Sharpe.

Hong, Lijian. 1999. "A Tale of Two Cities: A Comparative Study of the Political and Economic Development in Chengdu and Chongqing." In Jae Ho Chung, ed., *Cities in China: Recipes for Economic Development in the Reform Era,* 183–214. London: Routledge.

Hooper, Beverly. 2000. "Consumer Voices: Asserting Rights in Post-Mao China." *China Information* 14, no. 2: 92–128.

Huang, Philip. 1993. "'Public Sphere'/'Civil Society' in China?" *Modern China* 19, no. 2: 217–40.

Jie, Fan, and Wolfgang Taubmann. 2002. "Migrant Enclaves in Large Chinese Cities." In John R. Logan, ed., *The New Chinese City: Globalization and Market Reform,* 183–97. Oxford: Blackwell.

Jullien, François. 1995. *The Propensity of Things: Toward a History of Efficacy in China.* New York: Zone Books.

Kenworthy, Jeff, and Gang Hu. 2002. "Transport and Urban Change in Chinese Cities." *DISP* 151 (Zurich), 38, no. 4: 4–14.

Khan, Azizur Rahman, and Carl Riskin. 2001. *Inequality and Poverty in China in an Age of Globalization.* Oxford: Oxford University Press.

Kostof, Spiro. 1992. *The City Assembled: The Elements of Urban Form through History.* Boston: Little, Brown.

Lau, Pui-king. 1998. "Industry and Trade." In Y. M. Yeung and David K. Y. Chu, eds.,

Guangdong: Survey of a Province Undergoing Rapid Change, 127–50. 2d ed. Hong Kong: Chinese University Press.

Leaf, Michael. 2002. "A Tale of Two Villages: Globalization and Peri-Urban Change in China and Vietnam." *Cities* 19, no. 1: 23–31.

Leaf, Michael, and Daniel Abramson. 2002. "Global Networks, Civil Society, and the Transformation of the Urban Core in Quanzhou, China." In Eric H. Heikkila and Rafael Pizarro, eds., *Southern California in the World,* 153–78. Westport, Conn.: Praeger.

Lefebvre, Henri. 1968. *Le droit à la ville.* Paris: Anthropos.

Levy, Richard. 2003. "The Village Self-Government Movement: Elections, Democracy, the Party, and Anticorruption—Developments in Guandong." *China Information* 17, no. 1: 28–65.

Lewis, John Wilson. 1971. *The City in Communist China.* Stanford: Stanford University Press.

Li, Si-ming, and Wing-shing Tang, eds. 2000. *China's Regions, Polity, and Economy: A Study of Spatial Transformation in the Post-Reform Era.* Hong Kong: Chinese University Press.

Lin, George C. S. 1997. *Red Capitalism in South China.* Vancouver: University of British Columbia Press.

Lindau, Juan D., and Timothy Cheek, eds. 1998. *Market Economics and Political Change: Comparing China and Mexico.* Lanham, Md.: Rowman and Littlefield.

Linge, Godfrey, ed. 1997. *China's New Spatial Economy: Heading Towards 2020.* Hong Kong: Oxford University Press.

Link, Perry, Richard P. Madsen, and Paul G. Pickowicz, eds. 2002. *Popular China: Unofficial Culture in a Globalizing Society.* Lanham, Md.: Rowman and Littlefield.

Liu, Yi, Zhang Lei, and Godfrey Linge. 1997. "The Bohai Sea Rim: Some Development Issues." In Godfrey Linge, ed., *China's New Spatial Economy: Heading Towards 2020,* 123–43. Hong Kong: Oxford University Press.

Logan, John. 2002. *The New Chinese City: Globalization and Market Reform.* Oxford: Blackwell.

Luk, Chiu-ming. 1998. "Transport and Communication." In Y. M. Yeung and David K. Y. Chu, eds., *Guangdong: Survey of a Province Undergoing Rapid Change,* 329–54. 2d ed. Hong Kong: Chinese University Press.

Mallee, Hein. 1997. "Rural Household Dynamics and Spatial Mobility in China." In John R. Logan, ed., *The New Chinese City: Globalization and Market Reform,* 278–97. Oxford: Blackwell.

Marton, Andrew M. 2000. *China's Spatial Economic Development: Restless Landscapes in the Lower Yangzi Delta.* London: Routledge.

Maruya, Toyojiro. 1998. "The Economy." In Y. M. Yeung and David K. Y. Chu, eds., *Guandong: Survey of a Province Undergoing Rapid Change,* 63–86. 2d ed. Hong Kong: Chinese University Press.

Min, Ma. 2002. "Emergent Civil Society in the Late Qing Dynasty: The Case of

Suzhou." In David Faure and Tao Tao Liu, eds., *Town and Country in China: Identity and Perception*, 145–65. New York: Palgrave.

Mote, F. W. 1977. "The Transformation of Nanking, 1350–1400." In G. William Skinner, ed., *The City in Late Imperial China*, 101–54. Stanford, Calif.: Stanford University Press.

———. 1999. *Imperial China 900–1800*. Cambridge, Mass.: Harvard University Press.

Murphy, Rachel. 2002a. *How Migrant Labor Is Changing Rural China*. Cambridge: Cambridge University Press.

———. 2002b. "Return Migration, Entrepreneurship, and State-sponsored Urbanization in the Jiangxi Countryside." In John R. Logan, ed., *The New Chinese City: Globalization and Market Reform*, 229–44. Oxford: Blackwell.

Ng, Mee Kam. 2002. "Planning Cultures in Two Chinese Transitional Cities: Hong Kong and Shenzhen." Unpublished paper.

Ng, Mee Kam, Kervic Chan, and Peter Hills. 2002. "Sustainable Development in China: From Knowledge to Action." *International Journal of Environment and Sustainable Development* 2, no. 1: 36–61.

Ng, Mee Kam, and Wing Shing Tang. 2002. "Building a Modern Socialist City in an Age of Globalization: The Case of Shenzhen Special Economic Zone, People's Republic of China." In *Conference Proceedings: Theme 4: Globalization, Urban Transition and Governance in Asia, Forum on Urbanizing World and UN Urban Habitat II*, 117–37. New York: International Research Foundation for Development.

Oi, Jean C. 1999. *Rural China Takes Off: Institutional Foundations of Economic Reform*. Berkeley: University of California Press.

Ong, Aiwah. 1999. *Flexible Citizenship: The Cultural Logics of Transnationality*. Durham, N.C.: Duke University Press.

Peerenboom, R. P. 1993. "What's Wrong with Chinese Rights? Toward a Theory of Rights with Chinese Characteristics." *Harvard Human Rights Journal* 6: 29–57.

Pei, Minxin. 1998. "Chinese Civic Association: An Empirical Analysis." *Modern China* 24, no. 3: 285–318.

Perry, Elizabeth J., and Hsia-po Lü, eds. 1997. *Danwei: The Changing Urban Workplace in Historical and Comparative Perspective*. Armonk, N.Y.: M. E. Sharpe.

Portes, Alejandro, Manuel Castells, and Lauren A. Benton, eds. 1989. *The Informal Economy: Studies in Advanced and Less Developed Countries*. Baltimore: Johns Hopkins University Press.

Potter, Pitman B. 2003. *From Leninist Discipline to Socialist Legalism: Peng Zhen on Law and Political Authority in the PRC*. Stanford, Calif.: Stanford University Press.

Pye, Lucian. 1996. "The State and the Individual: An Overview Interpretation." In Brian Hook, ed., *The Individual and the State in China*, 16–42. Oxford: Clarendon Press.

Rocca, Jean-Louis. 2003. "The Rise of the Social and the Chinese State." *China Information* 17, no. 1: 1–27.

Rong, Chao-he, Li Wen-yan, Godrey Linge, and Dean Forbes. 1997. "Linking the Regions: A Continuing Challenge." In Godfrey Linge, ed., *China's New Spatial Economy: Heading Towards 2020,* 46–71. Hong Kong: Oxford University Press.

Rowe, William T. 1984. *Hankow: Commerce and Society in a Chinese City, 1796–1889.* Stanford, Calif.: Stanford University Press.

———. 1989. *Hankow: Conflict and Community in a Chinese City, 1796–1895.* Stanford, Calif.: Stanford University Press.

Rozman, Gilbert. 2003. "Center-Local Relations: Can Confucianism Boost Decentralization and Regionalism?" In Daniel A. Bell and Hahm Chaibong, eds., *Confucianism in the Modern World,* 181–200. New York: Cambridge University Press.

Said, Tony, and Xuedong Yang. 2003. "Innovations in China's Local Governance: Open Recommendation and Selection." *Pacific Affairs* 76, no. 2: 185–208.

Sassen, Saskia. 1991. *The Global City: New York, London, Tokyo.* Princeton, N.J.: Princeton University Press.

Shambaugh, David, ed. 2000. *Is China Unstable?* Armonk, N.Y.: M. E. Sharpe.

She, Zhixiang, Xu Guan, and Godfrey Linge. 1997. "The Head and Tail of the Dragon: Shanghai and Its Economic Hinterland." In Godfrey Linge, ed., *China's New Spatial Economy: Heading Towards 2020,* 98–122. Hong Kong: Oxford University Press.

Shi, Yilong. 1997. "One Model of Chinese Urbanization: The Urbanization Process in Xiamen City's Caitang Village." In Gregory Eliyu Guldin, ed., *Farewell to Peasant China: Rural Urbanization and Social Change in the Late Twentieth Century,* 123–50. Armonk, N.Y.: M. E. Sharpe.

Shiu, Sin-por, and Yang Chun. 2002. "A Study on Developing the Hong Kong–Shenzhen Border Zone." In Anthony Gar-on Yeh et al., eds., *Building a Competitive Pearl River Delta Region: Cooperation, Coordination, and Planning,* 245–70. Hong Kong: Centre for Urban Planning and Environmental Management, Hong Kong University.

Sinkule, Barbara J., and Leonard Ortolano. 1995. *Implementing Environmental Policy in China.* Westport, Conn.: Praeger.

Sit, Victor F. S. 1995. *Beijing: The Nature and Planning of a Chinese Capital City.* New York: John Wiley and Sons.

Skinner, G. William. 1977a. "Cities and the Hierarchies of Local Systems." In G. William Skinner, ed., *The City in Late Imperial China,* 275–351. Stanford, Calif.: Stanford University Press.

———. 1977b. "Regional Urbanization in Nineteenth-Century China." In G. William Skinner, ed., *The City in Late Imperial China,* 211–52. Stanford, Calif.: Stanford University Press.

———. 1977c. "Urban Development in Imperial China." In G. William Skinner, ed., *The City in Late Imperial China,* 3–32. Stanford, Calif.: Stanford University Press.

———. 1977d. "Urban Social Structure in Ch'ing China." In G. William Skinner, ed., *The City in Late Imperial China,* 521–54. Stanford, Calif.: Stanford University Press.

Skinner, G. William, ed. 1977. *The City in Late Imperial China*. Stanford, Calif.: Stanford University Press.

Smil, Vaclav. 1993. *China's Environmental Crisis: An Inquiry into the Limits of National Development*. New York: Praeger.

Solinger, Dorothy J. 1999. *Contesting Citizenship in Urban China: Peasant Migrants, the State, and the Logic of the Market*. Berkeley: University of California Press.

———. 2003. "Chinese Urban Jobs and the WTO." *China Journal* 49 (January): 61–88.

Steinhardt, Nancy Shatzman. 1990. *Chinese Imperial City Planning*. Honolulu: University of Hawai`i Press.

Strand, David. 1989. *Rickshaw Beijing: City People and Politics in the 1920s*. Berkeley: University of California Press.

———. 1999. "New Chinese Cities." In Joseph W. Esherick, ed., *Remaking the Chinese City: Modernity and National Identity, 1900–1950*, 211–24. Honolulu: University of Hawai`i Press.

Sum, Ngai-Ling. 2002. "Globalization and Hong Kong's Entrepreneurial City Strategies: Contested Visions and the Remaking of City Governance in (Post-)Crisis Hong Kong." In John R. Logan, ed., *The New Chinese City: Globalization and Market Reform*, 74–91. Oxford: Blackwell.

Taylor, John, and Qinghu Xie. 2000. "Wuhan: Policies for Management and Improvement of a Polluted City." In Terry Cannon, ed., *China's Economic Growth: The Impact on Regions, Migration, and the Environment*, 143–60. New York: St. Martin's Press.

Terrill, Ross. 1975. *Flowers on an Iron Tree: Five Cities of China*. Boston: Little, Brown.

Tomba, Luigi. 2004. "Creating an Urban Middle Class: Social Engineering in Beijing." *China Journal* 51: 1–26.

Tracy, Noel. 1997. "The Southeast: The Cutting Age of China's Economic Reform." In Godfrey Linge, ed., *China's New Spatial Economy: Heading Towards 2020*, 72–97. Hong Kong: Oxford University Press.

Tsin, Michael. 2000. "Canton Remapped." In Joseph W. Esherick, ed., *Remaking the Chinese City: Modernity and National Identity, 1900–1950*, 19–29. Honolulu: University of Hawai`i Press.

Tucker, Robert C., ed. 1978. *The Marx-Engels Reader*. 2d ed. New York: W. W. Norton.

Unger, Jonathan. 2002. *The Transformation of Rural China*. Armonk, N.Y.: M. E. Sharpe.

United Nations Centre for Human Settlement (Habitat). 2001. *Cities in a Globalizing World: Global Report on Human Settlements 2001*. London: Earthscan.

United Nations Department of Economic and Social Affairs. 1998. *World Urbanization Prospects: The 1996 Revision*. New York: United Nations.

Van Rooij, Benjamin. 2003. "Organization and Procedure in Environmental Law Enforcement: Sichuan in Comparative Perspective." *China Information* 17, no. 2: 36–64.

Vogel, Ezra F. 1989. *One Step Ahead in China: Guandong under Reform*. Cambridge, Mass.: Harvard University Press.

Wakeman, Frederick, Jr. 1993. "The Civil Society and Public Sphere Debate: Western Reflections on Chinese Political Culture." *Modern China* 19, no. 2 (April): 108–38.

Waley, Arthur. 1939. *Three Ways of Thought in Ancient China.* London: Allen and Unwin.

Wang Feng. 1997. "The Breakdown of a Great Wall: Recent Changes in the Household Registration System in China." In Thomas Sharping, ed., *Floating Population and Migration in China: The Impact of Economic Reforms,* 149–65. Mitteilungen des Instituts für Asienkunde, Hamburg, no. 284.

———. 2003. "Housing Improvement and Distribution in Urban China: Initial Evidence from China's 2000 Census." *China Review* 3, no. 2: 121–43.

Wang, Mark Yaolin. 2002. "Small City, Big Solution: China's Hukou System Reform and Its Potential Impacts." *DISP* 151 (Zurich), 38, no. 4: 23–29.

Wang, Shaoguang. 1995. "The Politics of Private Time: Changing Leisure Patterns in Urban China." In Deborah S. Davis et al., eds., *Urban Spaces in Contemporary China: The Potential for Autonomy and Community in Post-Mao China,* 149–72. Washington, D.C.: Woodrow Wilson Center Press and Cambridge University Press.

Wasserstrom, Jeffrey N. 1999. "Locating Old Shanghai: Having Fits about Where It Fits." In Joseph W. Esherick, ed., *Remaking the Chinese City: Modernity and National Identity, 1900–1950,* 192–210. Honolulu: University of Hawai`i Press.

Watt, John R. 1977. "The Yamen and Urban Administration." In G. William Skinner, ed., *The City in Late Imperial China,* 353–90. Stanford, Calif.: Stanford University Press.

Webster, Douglas, and Larissa Muller. 2002. "Challenges of Peri-urbanization in the Lower Yantze Region: The Case of the Hangzhou-Ningbo Corridor." Discussion paper. Asia Pacific Research Center, Stanford University.

Wei, Yehua Dennis. 2000. *Regional Development in China: State, Globalization, and Inequality.* London: Routledge.

Weston, Timothy B., and Lionel M. Jensen, eds. 2000. *China beyond the Headlines.* Lanham, Md.: Rowman and Littlefield.

Wheatley, Paul. 1971. *The Pivot of the Four Quarters: A Preliminary Enquiry into the Origins and Character of the Ancient Chinese City.* Edinburgh: Edinburgh University Press.

White, Gordon. 1996. "The Dynamics of Civil Society in Post-Mao China." In Brian Hook, ed., *The Individual and the State in China,* 196–222. Oxford: Clarendon Press.

White, Gordon, Jude Howell, and Xiaoyuan Shang. 1996. *In Search of Civil Society: Market Reform and Social Change in Contemporary China.* Oxford: Clarendon Press.

White, Lynn T., III. 1998a. *Unstately Power.* Vol. 1: *Local Causes of China's Economic Reforms.* Armonk, N.Y.: M. E. Sharpe.

———. 1998b. *Unstately Power.* Vol. 2: *Local Causes of China's Intellectual, Legal, and Governmental Reforms.* Armonk, N.Y.: M. E. Sharpe.

Wong, K. K., and X. B. Zhao. 1999. "The Influence of Bureaucratic Behavior on Land Apportionment in China: The Informal Process." *Environment and Planning C: Government and Policy* 17, no. 1: 113–26.

Wright, Arthur F. 1977. "The Cosmology of the Chinese City." In G. William Skinner, ed., *The City in Late Imperial China,* 33–74. Stanford, Calif.: Stanford University Press.

———. 1978. *The Sui Dynasty: The Unification of China, A.D. 581–617.* New York: Alfred A. Knopf.

Wu, Fulong. 2002. "China's Changing Urban Governance in the Transition towards a More Market-Oriented Economy." *Urban Studies* 39, no. 7: 1071–93.

Xu, Dixin, and Chengming Wu, eds. 2000. *Chinese Capitalism 1522–1840.* New York: St. Martin's Press.

Xu, Jiang, and Mee Kam Ng. 1998. "Socialist Planning in Transition: The Case of Guangzhou, China." *Third World Planning Review* 20, no. 1: 35–51.

Xu, Yinong. 2000. *The Chinese City in Space and Time: The Development of Urban Form in Suzhou.* Honolulu: University of Hawai`i Press.

Yan, Yunxiang. 2003. *Private Life under Socialism: Love, Intimacy, and Family in a Chinese Village, 1949–1999.* Stanford, Calif.: Stanford University Press.

Yang, Dali L. 1997. *Beyond Beijing: Liberalization and the Regions in China.* London: Routledge.

Yeh, Anthony Gar-on. 2002. "Further Cooperation between Hong Kong and the Pearl River Delta in Creating a More Competitive Region." In Anthony Gar-on Yeh et al., eds., *Building a Competitive Pearl River Delta Region: Cooperation, Coordination, and Planning,* 319–46. Hong Kong: Centre for Urban Planning and Environmental Management, Hong Kong University.

Yeh, Anthony Gar-on, and Fulong Wu. 1998. "The Urban Planning System in China." *Progress in Planning* 51, no. 3: 165–252.

Yeh, Anthony Gar-on, et al., eds. 2002. *Building a Competitive Pearl River Delta Region: Cooperation, Coordination, and Planning.* Hong Kong: Centre for Urban Planning and Environmental Management, Hong Kong University.

Yeung, Y. M., and David K. Y. Chu, eds. 1998. *Guangdong: Survey of a Province Undergoing Rapid Change.* 2d ed. Hong Kong: Chinese University Press.

Yeung, Y. M., and Yun-wing Sung, eds. 1996. *Shanghai: Transformation and Modernization under China's Open Policy.* Hong Kong: Chinese University Press.

Zhang, Li. 2001. *Strangers in the City: Reconfigurations of Space, Power, and Social Networks within China's Floating Population.* Stanford, Calif.: Stanford University Press.

Zhang, Li, Simon X. B. Zhao, and J. P. Tian. 2003. "Self-help in Housing and Chengzhongcun in China's Urbanization." *International Journal of Urban and Regional Research* 27, no. 4: 912–37.

Zhang, Tingwei. 2002a. "Challenges Facing Chinese Planners in Transitional China." *Journal of Planning Education and Research* 22, no. 1: 64–76.

———. 2002b. "Decentralization, Localization, and the Emergence of a Quasi-Participatory Decision-Making Structure in Urban Development in Shanghai." *International Planning Studies* 7, no. 4: 303–23.

Zhou, Min, and John R. Logan. 1996. "Market Transition and the Commodification of Housing in Urban China." *International Journal of Urban and Regional Research* 20, no. 3: 400–421.

Zhu, Yu. 1999. *New Paths to Urbanization in China: Seeking More Balanced Patterns*. Commack, N.Y.: Nova Science Publishers.

Index

John Friedmann is professor emeritus of the School of Public Policy and Social Research, University of California at Los Angeles, and honorary professor, University of British Columbia. He is the author of many books, including *The Prospect of Cities* (Minnesota, 2002).